CROSS AND CROWN

Thoughts for Lent
Christ's Sufferings
Christ the King

Rev. Fr. Robert Mäder

SARTO HOUSE

On the cover: The Crown of Charlemagne (the German Imperial Crown or Nuremberg Crown), used in the coronation of later German kings as Holy Roman Emperors. It was made during the 10th century at the workshops of the monastery at Reichenau.

SARTO HOUSE
PO Box 217
St. Marys, Kansas, 66536

ISBN   0-9639032-2-5

Library of Congress Catalog Card Number: 98-61890

First Printing—January 1999
Second Printing—December 2013
Third Printing—March 2018

CONTENTS

FOREWORD

Rev. Fr. Robert Mäder (1875-1945) came from the village of Wolfwil, Switzerland. He was ordainted priest in 1899. After serving as assistant in Biberist and pastor in Mümliswil, he was in 1912 chosen as first pastor of Holy Ghost Church in Basel, where he enjoyed the reputation of an outstanding pulpit orator. Fr. Mäder was co-founder of *Die Schildwache* (*The Sentinel*, a Catholic newspaper) and founder of the St. Theresa Middle School in Basel. The University of Fribourg granted him a doctoral degree *honoris causa*.

Fr. Robert Mäder was an uncompromising soldier of Christ, a fighter against all the spiritual evils of our times, especially against Modernism and every sort of deviation from Catholic doctrine and spirit. He was not only a great parish priest, but also a renowned and respected author, an untiring fighter against Nazism, Communism and all the poisonous modern ideologies that deny the kingship of Jesus Christ, a Swiss patriot and an exemplary leader of Catholic Action.

As one might expect from such an energetic personality, Fr. Mäder's language is tough, hard-hitting, honest and direct. He belonged to the classic type of home missionary which the German-speaking peoples call a "penance-preacher." However, behind the skilled, pulpit-pounding rhetoric stood a man of solid theology, wide learning and deep prayer.

Thoughts For Lent

You Must Think!

Life from birth to death is a continual test in which the Great Examiner, God, thoroughly and patiently, wisely and searchingly, tests man, to see how this creature of His stands in relation to Him, his Creator and Redeemer. To see whether he is seeking his eternal good in Him or in himself. To see whether this work of His hands will opt for Him or for His opponent, Satan. Our little existence on this little earth, with our little joys and sorrows, our little words and deeds, has no other value and no other purpose.

Such thoughts never come into our consciousness so forcefully as in Lent. *Lent is a time of examination.* And Easter, with its Easter confession and Easter communion, is the capstone of the season and the final examination. To see whether we are ready for heaven or for hell. Because there is absolutely no third choice. Either we are ready for the Lord or we are ready for the devil. Examination time is always a serious time. It concerns the future. And here it is an eternal future. Lent should not be a time in the Church year which goes by without leaving any mark at all upon us. It must be an intimate personal experience.

First of all it is a time when we learn to think Catholic again. Man is man because he thinks. In this way man differs from the whole of material creation, from the inanimate world, from the world of plants and animals. Inanimate objects do not think. Plants do not think. Animals do not think. Man thinks. Furthermore, men differ among themselves: there are pagans, because some men think as materialists. There are Christians, because some men think like Christ. There are Catholics because some men think like the Catholic Church. What specifies and differentiates man in the first place is his thinking. Man is what he thinks.

We must make another distinction. There are men who begin a thought but do not carry it through to its final conclusion. They lack logic. Consistency. They pray the Catholic Profession of Faith (the Creed). But the Faith lives in them only on an unconscious level. As if they were half asleep. In their conscious life, it is as if they were pagans. Their daily thoughts are never—or at least seldom—concerned with God, Christ, Church, eternity, but rather with eating, drinking, working, playing, sleeping. These people have eyes but see not, ears but hear not. In other words, they are Catholics who do not think Catholic.

These Catholics today form a majority. Religious ignorance, Cardinal Mermillod has written, is one of the most terrible facts of modern life. "Thoughts of the supernatural—who has them? They hardly exist any more." Daily life is dominated by materialist, liberal and socialist ideas, not by Catholic ideas. Take any hour of any day. How much of the supernatural do you find in it? How much thought for the presence of God? How much reflection on eternity? On the Blessed Sacrament? On Christ Crucified? On Our Lady? Mermillod was right: supernatural thinking these days is practically non-existent. That is one of the reasons why Catholicism has so little impact. Catholic ideas are no longer in the air. "The truth is diminishing among the children of men" (Ps. 11:2).

So what should we do? People must be brought back to Catholic thinking, to Catholic after-thinking. But how does this come about? Through Catholic fore-thinking.[1]

Through preaching on the great, eternal truths: God, Christ, Church, eternity. By constantly coming back to the fundamentals: to the one thing needful, the one thing that saves us: that we are on the earth to know God, to love Him, to serve Him, and in this way get to heaven. That we are either saved or damned and that there is no third option. That mortal sin is the greatest possible misfortune. That faith is necessary for salvation. That we do nothing of any val-

---

[1] Mgr. Mäder here coins a word, *vordenken* ("to fore-think") as a parallel to the common German verb *nachdenken* ("to reflect," literally "to after-think"). A good example of his unique, distinctive style.

ue without grace. That outside the Church there is no salvation. This is what Lent means: to fore-think the great, eternal truths for the people.

But fore-thinking is not enough. To the fore-thinking of the preacher and writer must be added the after-thinking of the listener and reader. Many forget this. Perhaps most. The sermon does not end with the Amen. Any more than the meal is over with the cooking of the dinner. One must also eat! One must assimilate the truth. One must digest it and absorb it into one's flesh and blood. One must make it part of his own spiritual possessions. For this reason Christ compared the truth with bread: "Man does not live by bread alone, but by every word that proceeds from the mouth of God" (Mt. 4:4).

Hence the necessity of reflection, *i.e.*, meditative penetrating into the divine truth. It is not enough to have heard the truth once. If you hear it only once, you forget it. You must not forget what you have heard, but hold it securely in memory. But that can happen only if you let the truth become fixed in your inmost soul, so that you can be always coming back to it. Only a truth thought out is a truth possessed. Only a truth possessed is a living and vigorous truth. The pulpit speaker works in vain if he does not succeed in bringing his hearers to a minimum of reflection, *i.e.*, to serious after-thinking.

The mother of St. John Bosco once took into her home a working-class boy, poor and soaked to the skin. She gave him hospitality, went through his night prayers with him and then gave him a couple of good thoughts to ponder before he went to sleep. Later, in Don Bosco's houses the day never ended without the superior of the house giving his charges a good thought. This is the minimum of meditation: never to go to sleep without a good thought. And whoever is resolved to do more than the minimum will say to himself: Never a morning, never a day without a quarter of an hour, or ten minutes, or at least five minutes, of serious prayerful meditation on some religious truth. That is especially what Sunday is for. Sunday is a day not for scattering, but for gathering. A day for thinking. Thinking about things, thinking through things, thinking to conclusions.

Our first Lenten resolution will therefore be: We must do more thinking! Less scattering and more gathering! No day without a minimum of meditation! No evening without a good thought before going to sleep! And about reading: Read books by authors who think! As for human society: Associate with people who think! Empty-headedness has brought human society to the brink of destruction. As Beda Weber once said: "Thinking by halves leads to the devil. Total thinking, however, leads to God."

I add to that: Total thinking leads to Christ. Total thinking leads to the Church. Total thinking leads to Rome. Total thinking leads to heaven. Total thinking is rational thinking. Total thinking is Christian thinking. Total thinking is Catholic thinking!

YOU MUST PRAY!

The first Lenten resolution was: You must think! You must think Catholic. Because every problem of the individual and of nations for the past five hundred years stems from the fact that Catholic thinking is no longer understood; and conversely, all renewal of the individual and of the people begins when we learn to think Catholic again. We consider it the chief assignment of our life constantly to call attention to this self-evident principle, without which all Catholicism is sounding brass and tinkling cymbal.

The second self-evident principle is this: *You must pray!* Earlier ages called man the *animal religiosum.* The praying being. Man is a living being which thinks and prays. If you don't think, you don't pray. If you don't pray, you don't think. Not to pray is always a sign of spiritual weakness. A drift toward the world of the irrational. The animal is a living being which does not pray, because it is a living being which does not think. This is what brands neo-paganism, with its hatred of prayer, as spiritual emptiness.

Lent is a school of prayer. Teaching us to kneel down and fold our hands. To cry out to God. Lent begins with Ash Wednesday. Ash Wednesday with its ashes on the forehead and its reminder: "Remember, man, that thou art dust and unto dust thou shalt return." It teaches man to pray by showing him what he is. Man is a mortal being.

Man comes and goes. He comes if and when Another wishes. Without being asked. He goes away again, if and when Another wishes. Here, too, without being asked whether he wants to or not, he has to. What does this mean? Man is a dependent being. An *ens ab alio,* as the philosophers say, a being from and through and for Another. This Other is God. Mankind without God is unthinkable.

Nothing brings this total dependence on God so forcefully to mind as hunger. The Gospel tells us that the Savior after fasting forty days, was hungry. What is hunger? A sign that man, as an *ens ab alio,* a dependent being, needs God. A sign that man is not self-sufficient. A sign that he must pray. Hunger seems to be something so essential to mankind that we could almost say: Man is a being who hungers and must therefore pray.

Hunger is therefore that mysterious longing for nourishment, strength, fulfillment, which every creature experiences. The whole of creation hungers. The earth hungers for life-giving rain, fire for fuel, the plant for water, the flower for the sun. Man's body hungers for bodily food, his understanding for knowledge, his heart for love. Hunger shows us that, along with a dependent being, there must be an Independent Being; alongside helplessness, an Almighty; alongside neediness, a Helper. Hunger is a proof instilled in man for the existence of Divine Providence.

Modern liberal man no longer believes in the *ens ab alio.* He considers himself independent. As a being who exists for himself, through himself and for himself. Something, therefore, like God. Modern man does not believe in hunger any longer. And because he no longer believes in hunger, he no longer believes in the necessity of prayer. What does God do? He sends an economic crisis (a depression). He sends unemployment in industrialized countries. He sends confusion to the learned and helplessness to the powerful.

And what does all this mean? It means that man, in spite of all technical and scientific progress, is a being who is hungry. A being who needs God. The whole meaning of the depression is that it is a lesson from God. Hunger makes men humble again. Hunger reminds us of the saying in the Gospel, "Without Me you can do nothing." Hunger brings powerlessness back to the divine All-Powerfulness. The depression is something sent by Divine Providence—

a great obligatory Lent, embracing all people without distinction of religion.

The purpose of this Lent is also to be a school of prayer. Hungry people must learn to pray again. Because need teaches prayer. An example of this school of prayer is the wandering of the people of God in the desert in the Old Testament. God wanted to fashion into a new people this great throng which had lost its courage and its character through long oppression. So He imposed a forty-year Lent on the people He had miraculously freed from Egypt.

Hunger is a great revealer. It shows what is in man. One it makes a revolutionary, a murmurer, a fault-finder with God and an agitator of the people. Another it brings to his knees, to fold his hands and pray. And God heard their cry and gave them miraculous manna all the days of their wandering. And the people again realized: the bread comes from God!

So it goes again today! The depression can have a double effect: some will run away, others will pray. Some will despair and say: "What shall we eat, and what shall we drink, and wherewith shall we be clothed?" Others will conquer the crisis in the light of the words of Christ: "Your Father knows that you need all these things." They seek first the Kingdom of God and His justice. And all else will be added unto them. Lent—the ordinary liturgical season in which we now are, and the extraordinary season of a depression—is therefore a time of decision.

This double period of fasting must be for us a school of prayer. Hunger will draw us back to God. To God from Whom all bread comes. Material, spiritual and Eucharistic. For the individual and for the people. We will be, much more than in the past, thinking and praying beings. We will not think of bread except in connection with God. Praying. Thanking. And we will do this especially when we are enjoying the good things of God. Let us pray always as Christ wishes (Lk. 18:1), but especially let us never forget to pray when we eat, *i.e.*, when we satisfy our hunger.

Mealtime is a festive hour of deep religious character in the life of all ancient peoples. Praying before eating was always a sign of civilization. Eating without praying was considered barbaric. Eating and praying belonged together in all civilized nations. Only two kinds of beings were recognized. One was the animal, which ate without praying (this included those who put themselves on the level of animals). Thinking man cannot eat without humbly recognizing that he is not self-sufficient and thankfully remembering where all good things come from. The decline in prayer before meals is an ominous first step toward a decline in religion as a whole.

Lent as a time of prayerful hunger is Christocentric. It wishes to bring us to the awareness that the Christian never prays alone but always *per Dominum nostrum Jesum Christum!* Through Our Lord Jesus Christ. Through the Redeemer and His Precious Blood. This is what gives meaning to all our prayers. Especially the great prayers in times of serious trouble for humanity. This is the lesson of the entire Old and New Testaments.

The Blood of the Lamb must go with us, if our plea is to reach the throne of God. I know of no prayer better suited to express the spirit of Lent and become, daily and hourly, more and more the cry of mankind, than the *Parce, Domine*. Spare, O Lord, spare Thy people, whom Thou hast redeemed by Thy Precious Blood. Let us pray in a Christocentric way. With the voice of the Precious Blood: Lord God, give us bread. Our daily bread and Eucharistic Bread.

YOU MUST FAST!

We cannot speak about Lent without speaking about fasting.[2] Now fasting is not at all popular. There seems to be something faintly reactionary about it. Something medieval. And modern man wants to live. To live fully. Fasting seems like putting a restriction on living.

The Church has a different outlook. She sees in fasting not something negative, but something positive. Not something limiting, but something constructive. Something healthful and health-giving. Something strong and strengthening. She does not mourn,

---

[2] This sentence depends for its full impact on another wordplay impossible to render in standard English. "Lent" in German is *Fastenzeit,* literally "fasting time." The idea is therefore, "We cannot speak about fasting time without speaking about fasting."

but rather rejoices, when Lent comes round. The Preface for Lent is a veritable hymn of praise to abstinence and renunciation.

"It is truly right and just," it sings, "proper and holy, that we give thanks always and everywhere to Thee, Holy Lord, Almighty Father, Eternal God. Through bodily fasting you curb our vices, raise our spirit, and bestow virtue and reward. Through Christ Our Lord." Lent is a spring tonic for body and soul. Lent is a rebirth and resurrection. The healthfulness of Lent has a thousand years of successful testing behind it. We have said man is a being who gets hungry and therefore must eat. And now we must add a little correction: man is a being who must also fast.

The first mandate for fasting does not come from a bishop. The first mandate for fasting comes directly from God. It is in the first chapter of Genesis. It belongs to the oldest and most venerable proclamations to mankind: "Behold. I have given you all plants and all trees for food....From every tree of the garden you may eat...everything that lives and grows, you may eat." But God added, "But from the tree of the knowledge of good and evil you may not eat. For on the day you eat of it, you will die." Two great commandments appear, therefore, on the threshold of human history. Man dies if he does not eat. But man also dies if he refuses to fast.

The public ministry of Jesus begins by stressing this law of fasting. Christ fasts in the name of the new humanity for forty days and forty nights. And He expressly says: "Man does not live by bread alone, but by every word that comes from the mouth of God." Along with the right to eat goes the duty not to eat, *i.e.*, to fast. Both are necessary for man to remain man. Today's fasting requirements demand (in view of human weakness) only a minimum of fasting, but in this minimum it is urgently stressed that a certain minimum of fasting is indispensable for Christianity.

Fasting "uplifts the spirit." Man consists of two parts. One he takes from the world of the spirit. The other he takes from the material world. A body and a soul. He is and remains human on the condition that he gives to the soul what belongs to the soul, and to the body what belongs to the body. The soul should not let the body starve. The body, on the other hand, should not overpower the soul.

The danger, since the Garden of Eden, is usually not from above downwards, but rather from below upwards. Normally the body tyrannizes over the soul, not the soul over the body. Normally the body claims the first attention in man, claims the lead in right and power. Fasting, on the other hand, underscores the primacy of the spirit over the body, in that it gives the last word, from a will enlightened by faith, over the quantity and quality of food, on the how much and the what of nourishment.

Fasting is therefore, first of all, a question of principle. It makes eating and drinking more a question of conscience than of the stomach. As important as eating is, it is never the thing of first importance, but rather second or third. For the people as for the individual. We do not live to eat! We eat only to live—indeed, to live in time and in eternity. We may not take the means and make them an end. That would be gluttony. Yet that is usually what we find in contemporary humanity. Here, there, everywhere, people live to eat.

The entire world scene today revolves around economics. People engage in outside activity in order to earn money, and they earn money in order to eat. "Let us eat and drink, for tomorrow we die" (Is. 22:13). *Panem et circenses,* cried the ancients, and moderns say the same thing. Food and entertainment! Fasting says: God and the soul above all! The first thing is to be human and to be Christian. Then, as human and Christian, *sub specie aeternitatis et divinitatis,* in light of God and of eternity—eat and be merry.

Fasting makes for a stronger will. The stomach has become a revolutionary as a result of our fall from grace; it throws all caution to the winds. It is one of the seven chief sinners in the kingdom of Man. Egotist. Heartless toward the poor. Lazy. Irresponsible. The stomach does not like to pray. The stomach does not even hesitate to steal if it has to. It is a worshipper of idols. It is ready to betray God and conscience, faith and eternity for the sake of food. And the more it is allowed, the more brazen it gets. A reckless tyrant. And the will becomes its weak, cringing slave.

There is no way to bring the enslaved will back to independence except through abstinence and renunciation. This is especially true in the use of alcohol. Abstinence and renunciation give man back to man, in that they give his will back to him. We talk about training the will through gymnastics and sports. We talk about race and blood. But we know that is usually all forgotten when the beast of pleasure-seeking rises up in the stomach. We must resort to the tried and true remedies. The beast of pleasure-seeking will become tame only when we let it get hungry. The best training ground for the will is the training ground of fasting.

Fasting is healthy. This much is certain: all illness and all death are the result of the breaking of the first law of fasting in the Garden of Eden. If Adam and Eve had kept the first law of fasting, the world would be a paradise today. Quite apart from that, the great apostle of a healthy mankind, Joseph de Maistre,[3] dares to claim: "If we could avoid entirely every kind of extreme, we could avoid most illnesses. More people die from overeating than are killed in wars."

The Roman philosopher Seneca described the age of Nero, "We should not be surprised at the countless illnesses. Just count the cooks." And Maistre adds, "Everyone who seriously asks himself the question, will be convinced that he eats twice as much as he should."

This much is certain: in spite of having wandered around on the earth for six thousand years, mankind still does not understand the great art of eating. Neither in regard to how much nor in regard to what. The purpose of fasting is to bring us back to this fine art. Through abstinence to a correct choice of foods. Through renunciation to correct proportions.

Our first resolution for Lent was, Lord, teach us to think! And the second: Lord, teach us to pray! We must now add: Lord, teach us how to eat! Lord, teach us to fast! Lord, teach us to eat as though fasting!

YOU MUST GIVE ALMS!

Yes indeed—Christians must learn to think more. If they think more, they will also pray more. But prayer, important as it is, is not all it takes to become holy. Ascetical practices also belong to the spiritual life. To prayer must be added fasting. Even then, Christ said to those who were praying and fasting: "If your justice does not

---

[3] French philosopher, diplomat and statesman (1753-1821).

exceed that of the Scribes and Pharisees, you will not enter the king-dom of heaven." The Pharisees observed the externals of the Law—rules for fasting and Mosaic ceremonial—down to the smallest de-tail. And yet they overlooked the main thing they needed in order to recognize the Messias: freedom from material cares. The God of Christianity is Spirit, and those who worship Him must worship in truth and spirit. Whoever wants to be a Christian must first free himself of material concerns.

This is just what Lent is all about. And for that purpose it uses three things above all. After prayer and fasting, which we have al-ready considered, almsgiving must be added to complete the pic-ture. We read in the Book of Tobias, "It is better to give alms than to treasure up gold" (12:8). Almsgiving is right up front in Christ's program. We must conquer the Pharisee in ourselves so that the Christian can shine through.

Almsgiving has a double educational value: religious and social. There was once an Anglican bishop who came to see the truth. His mind became Catholic. But in order to make the transfer to the Catholic Church, he would have had to give up his very large in-come. That was something he could not do. It was something he didn't want to do. His heart remained Protestant. A friend of his who had recently become Catholic tried tactfully to point out to him the central problem. The friend took a sheet of paper and wrote the word "God." "What do you see on this sheet?" he asked the puzzled prelate. "Simply 'God.'" Then the friend covered the word with a gold coin. "Can you still see that word?" he asked the bishop, who answered by hanging his head. He understood. His conscience forced him to admit it: Between me and the truth stands a barrier of gold. Wealth is preventing me from believing. My head acknowledges the truth of Catholicism; my heart denies it. How right Pascal was when he said, *Le coeur a ses raisons que la raison ne connait pas*—The heart has its reasons that reason knows not of.

What a powerful role money has played in the history of reli-gion in the course of the centuries! Judaism awaited a Messias. But a Messias of great riches and vast political power. They could not understand a poor Christ. Between Judaism and Christianity stands the wall of mammon.

No one can serve two masters. Judaism opted for mammon and against Christianity. In the decision for or against Christ, money plays a decisive part. The same is true in many respects for the great break with the Faith in the sixteenth century and for the modern apostasy implicit in capitalism and the religion of the proletariat. The grounds are not intellectual; they are predominantly economic.

The educational function of almsgiving consists in freeing man for the service of God, in that it gives him freedom from money. To build up this freedom from dependence on money and possessions, to being what we call "poor in spirit," was the main thing Jesus tried to teach His followers. Nothing seemed closer to His heart.

Thus a famous sociologist could write in the spirit of Christianity, "The proper struggle of modern man is not material; rather, it is the moral struggle against money. Man must subject it to himself, not himself to it. It is a holy war and at the same time an acutely social problem. It is a fight of the spiritual against the unspiritual. Simply it is a question of God against the devil." But if almsgiving is going to be a truly spiritual war of independence, then clearly almsgiving must not be merely shadow-boxing, but rather a body-blow. A sacrifice that hurts.

The other educational function of almsgiving is social. You could substitute the word "neighbor" for "God" in the conversion story of the Anglican bishop, and it would be just as valid. Money prevents us from seeing our neighbor, as it prevents us from seeing God. Money is egocentric. We call it private property. Christianity has always protected private property against Communism and Socialism. But Christianity has also always stressed the social dimension of private property over against capitalism and economic liberalism.

The great Archbishop of Constantinople, John Chrysostom, that giant among preachers, points to the first epistle to the Corinthians when he speaks of giving, and of giving thanks, when he says, "*Mine* and *thine* are mere words. Everything belongs to the Creator. And because it does not belong to us but to the Lord, we must turn it to the use of our fellowman. You and your fellowman have everything in common, as the sun, the air and the earth and everything else is common. Whatsoever one has received, he must share. No one to whom something has been given, may keep it all to himself. Whatever one keeps for his own exclusive and selfish use, becomes someone else's property." These and similar thoughts are not bolshevik, but primitive Christian wisdom. Having and giving go together.

Out of this commonality of private property arises the duty of almsgiving. "In Christian society," says the economist Ratzinger, "everyone must give. He who has much must give much; another must give from that little which he calls his own." I stress the words *everyone must* and *he who has much must give much*. Charity is not a matter of feeling but of conscience.

It is not dictated by conscience to give little to one and handsomely to another. But it is dictated by conscience to give as a general principle. It is not a duty in justice toward the individual, but it is a duty of justice as a general principle. In this sense, and only in this sense, was Proudhon[4] right, and we have seen St. John Chrysostom say: "Private property leads to theft." Whoever does not give according to what belongs to him, is stealing.

Giving is an act of charity (in the sense of Christian love). The value of the sacrifice depends not merely on the size of the gift, but on the intention and attitude of the giver. You know the moving story of the poor widow: "Jesus sat opposite the treasury and watched the multitude putting money into it. Many rich people put in large sums. And a poor widow came and put in two copper coins which make a penny. And he called his disciples to him and said to them, 'Truly, I say to you, this poor widow has put in more than all those who are contributing to the treasury. For they all contributed out of their abundance; but she out of her poverty has put in everything she had, her whole living'" (Mk. 12:42-44).

The foundation of society is justice. One clean hand in transaction with another. But the crowning fulfillment of society is charity. The open hand. In a society in which everyone uses for his own development only what he needs and puts the surplus at the disposal of the group, no one will ever be in want. And here the "power of little things" is striking. "The small donations of the poor are more important in society than the gifts of the rich. Wherever it

---

[4]   French economist (1809-1865).

comes to works of charity, the contributions of the little people are the main thing in a material and economic sense" (Ratzinger).

YOU MUST DO PENANCE!

Whoever say "A" must also say "B." Whoever thinks must also pray. Whoever prays must also fast and give alms. But even that is not enough. He must also become a new man. Lent achieves its ultimate purpose in the Easter confession and Easter communion. Easter, the Resurrection—that is the new man. But this does not happen without a struggle. Because there are two men in each of us. The old man and the new man. And the new man can prevail only if he succeeds in throwing out the old. To accomplish this is the work of penance. And that means penance as conversion and penance as seriousness of life.

The word *penance* is one of those words which is no longer found in the vocabulary of modern man. It is considered old-fashioned and is eschewed in the lifestyle of the well-educated and refined. We hardly ever see it even in religious literature, which gives a one-sided emphasis to the message of joy. And yet we must do the one and cannot leave the other out. Gospel and penance go together. Was not Jesus' entire life one of uninterrupted penance from the manger to the Cross? Did Christ not say, "Whoever wishes to be my disciple, let him deny himself, take up his cross, and follow me" (Mt. 16:24)?

Penance means, first of all, conversion. According to St. Thomas, sin is a turning away from God and to creatures. Conversion is a turning away from creatures and back to God. A return to God as Creator and Lawgiver, standard and goal of men. We call confession a conversion, but that is not the heart of the matter. Confession is necessary but secondary. The main thing is an interior transformation, a turning from a disordered attachment to creatures and a return to God in contrition and purpose of amendment. A confession which does not include this is a self-deception and a joke.

Confession is conversion in action and has unavoidable social dimensions. Isaias, in his Chapter 58, preached a scathing sermon to the pious of his day—a sermon which in this connection is very timely today. "Cry aloud, spare not, lift up your voice like a trumpet; declare to my people their transgression. They seek me daily; they delight to draw near to God." (They are, therefore, devout people, regular churchgoers. People who practice acts of piety, even fasting.)

And how does their piety, their Easter, work itself out in practice? Listen to the prophet: "Behold, in the day of your fast you seek your own pleasure, and oppress all your workers. Behold, you fast only to quarrel and to fight and to hit with wicked fist. Fasting like yours will not make your voice to be heard on high. Is such the fast that I choose, a day for a man to humble himself? Is it to bow down his head like a rush, and to spread sackcloth and ashes under him? Will you call this a fast, and a day acceptable to the Lord? Is not this the fast that I choose: to loose the bonds of wickedness, to undo the thongs of the yoke, and let the oppressed go free, and to break every yoke? Is it not to share your bread with the hungry, and bring the homeless poor into your house; when you see the naked, to cover him, and not to hide yourself from your own flesh? Then you shall call, and the Lord will answer; you shall cry, and he will say, here I am. The Merciful. The Lord your God."

This is what makes a Christian Easter in the face of a Communist proletariat and the threat of world revolution. This is the new man coming out of the confessional. Only by receiving the sacrament like that can we make an impression on the non-Catholic world. The raw number of communions counted up and tallied statistically—this is not what makes the real impression, but rather the social awareness of those converting after their Easter confession and Communion in their families, awareness of others in their parish community, awareness of their fellowman. Conversion is not only a return to God, but also a return to one's neighbor in the sense of the great commandment.

Penance is also seriousness of life. Anyone who has once observed Lent in a really spiritual way, looks on life and the world with different eyes. With the eyes of faith on original sin and on the passion of Our Lord. A look into the distance toward death and judgment and eternity. Under the pressure of world-wide need and the threat of total collapse. In this light must we consider the pursuit of pleasure in this world. Even Catholic pleasure. When we do that, it becomes like dancing in a burning house. Stupid. Unnatural. In-

sane. Criminal. Christianity may be happy, but it cannot be frivolous.

What we need today is a Noah, a Jeremiah, a John the Baptist,
a Vincent Ferrer, a St. Francis, someone to summon us to penance.
Like the prophet who, after the murder of God on Golgotha, ran
through the streets of Jerusalem night and day, shouting, "Voice of
the East, Voice of the West, Voice of the four winds, Voice against
Jerusalem and against the Temple, Voice against the whole people.
Woe! Woe! Penance! Penance! Penance!" Christians must again re-
alize that theirs is the religion of the Crucified. Let us have more seriousness! More simplicity! More spirit of sacrifice!

And this spirit of penance, this seriousness of life, we must
preach also to the young people. There are two ways of teaching:
The way of the Gospel and the way of the world. The way of the
Gospel is founded on the principle: Duty before pleasure! The
world, on the other hand, says: As little self-control and sacrifice as
possible! Pleasure! Enjoyment of life! Luxuries. Sentimentality. Naturalism. Experience shows every day how far we get with that kind
of program. A youth that is healthy and strong-willed is unthinkable without the old regimen of *sustine et abstine* (persevere and
learn to do without), without the spirit of endurance and abstinence. This is the exercise we need above all. That is the thing of
first importance that we need to do. As St. Paul says, "Every athlete
exercises self-control in all things. I must chastise my body and
bring it into subjection."

And thus we come to another side of the problem of penance.
There is not only a defensive in penance, but also an offensive. Endurance and abstinence are defensive. Chastisement is offensive. It
is based on a Pauline principle: "Those who belong to Christ have
crucified their flesh with its passions and desires" (Gal. 5:24). Ascetical practices we call mortifications. Mortification has nothing
to do with morticians. Reasonable mortification does not go contrary to the requirements of good health. Mortification has as its
goal simply to tame the rebellious body and to do it by means of
something that hurts.

The saints have a whole arsenal of offensive weapons of penance: hair-shirts, belts, chains, and disciplines. We moderns have
laid down our arms in this respect. It is not necessary to go as far as

all that. One should—in fact—do nothing without the permission of one's spiritual director. Penance is inventive. You will find other means of reaching your goal of taming the body. And if we don't find them, God always finds them for us. The pedagogy of pain does not create any medicine quite out of this world. It belongs to the school of divine teaching. Through bodily pain to the healing and sanctification of the soul!

He who has ears to hear, let him hear! Not everyone hears the sermon on penance. Only those to whom God gives the grace. Penance must begin with the righteous. In the decisive times such as we are now in, it is a matter above all of good people being converted. Not the Freemasons, not the Socialists, not the Jews, not the Communists. Not them, but us. And to do that, we must begin by setting an example for others of a more serious Christianity, less conformed to the ways of the world. Whatever the world may say to the contrary, we must do penance.

BACK TO THE POOR, HUMBLE, CRUCIFIED JESUS CHRIST

The high point of Lent is Christ on the cross. The Crucified Christ is the sum and substance of Christianity, so that St. Paul can say, "I decided to know nothing among you except Jesus Christ and Him crucified" (I Cor. 2:2). The crucifixion is therefore also the main thing we should preach in our time. The most important, the most necessary and the most urgent for people today.

Around the turn of the century there was much talk about the reform of Catholicism. It was thought that the Church must be more progressive, contemporary, open to the world. New ways must be found to reach the people, replacing the well trodden paths of yesterday. Then a Benedictine, Fr. Godehard Geiger, came along and wrote a pamphlet called "Back to the Poor, Humble, Crucified Savior Jesus Christ."

To reform, he said, means to refurbish and renew the original form, the original spirit. Now the original spirit of the Church is the spirit of Jesus Christ, as it appears in the Gospels, the spirit of renunciation, of the cross, and of sacrifice, as revealed in the life and ministry and teachings of Jesus—therefore the spirit of the poor, humble, crucified Savior Jesus Christ.

There is no Christianity except the Christianity of Christ. And the Christianity of Christ is simply Christ Himself, Christ as the Way, the Truth and the Life. The living Christ. Christ as Person and Mystery. Christ as Head and Christ in His members. It is most appropriate in this connection to repeat the words of the superior general of a religious order, who was asked to make major changes in his congregation: *"Aut sum ut sum aut non sum!"*—"Either I am what I am, or I am not." Either Christianity is Christ, or there is no Christianity.

The Christianity of Christ is redemption through the God-Man. The religion of grace. Of supernatural life and supernatural help. Divine grace is everything in the kingdom of God and in souls. Everything else in the world has meaning for the kingdom of God only insofar as it can be made into a tool of grace by the good will of man. Christ formulates this rule of the kingdom of God in the clearest possible way in the parable of the vine and the branches: "Without me you can do nothing." As Fr. Geiger says: "All the works of God arise *ex nihilo* and precisely in that way show themselves to be works of God." Human nothingness becomes the seal of divine grace.

For this reason Christ, in going about the work of our redemption and the founding of the Church, renounced all those things which men use in their human schemes to do great things in the world. In order to bring the Redemption to its fulfillment, He needed only human nature and the things that human nature finds necessary for its existence—something to eat every day and clothes to wear—but He used these things only as something to offer to His heavenly Father. What He did not use, what He rejected in principle, was possession of earthly things, the power and splendor of earthly things, the enjoyment of earthly life.

Christ was poor. He was born in a shelter for animals. His cradle was a feed-trough. He spent the first years of His life in exile. His daily bread was the modest income from working with His hands and later the donations of devout people. During the three years of His public ministry He had no home. The foxes have dens and the birds have their nests, but the Son of Man has nowhere to lay His head. And finally He hangs on a cross; even His clothes are taken away, and He is buried in another man's tomb. Christ is poor.

Because the Church is the continuation of Christ, the Church must be poor. In His instructions to the Apostles, Jesus said, "Take no gold, nor silver, nor copper in your belts, no bag for your journey...nor two tunics, nor sandals, nor a staff" (Mt. 10:9). Now of course the Church and her priests need a certain number of earthly goods and services to accomplish their mission, but only as means to an end. Only what is necessary. Whoever has only what he needs is poor.

A contemporary writer speaks of a special "original sin" in Catholic people. He calls it "too much fat." We must go into training to attack the fat—not to kill it, as Luther did; not to disguise it, as so many people try to do these days; but simply to get rid of it. In fighting fat it helps to exercise, to stimulate the circulation, to strengthen the nerves, to get back to simple foods. In Catholicism today, we must stop boasting—as we sometimes do—about our fat.

It is not good for the Church to be fat. When she cannot bring her inner strength to bear on slimming down, then God from time to time allows the slimming (in the interest of health) to take place through political violence or revolution. What is wrong is always wrong, but it can become a *felix culpa*. God knows how to take the sins of nations and peoples and put them to use for the good of the Church. She comes out younger, more vigorous and stronger.

Christ was humble. The basic error which has found its way into men's heads since the Garden of Eden is that they think they are gods. Christ considered it His first duty to correct this error. "Though He was in the form of God, He did not count equality with God a thing to be grasped, but emptied Himself, taking the form of a slave, being born in the likeness of men. And being found in human form he humbled Himself and became obedient unto death, even death on a cross." Thus says St. Paul to the Philippians (2:6-8). The most important thing that a man must learn from other men is that he is nothing of himself. He is the littlest. And this littleness as the fundamental truth of man Jesus exemplified from the manger to the Cross.

Humility must become therefore also the basic law of Christianity. Paul puts this idea into wonderful shape in his first epistle to the Corinthians: "Consider your call, brethren; not many of you were wise according to worldly standards, not many were powerful, not many were of noble birth; but God chose what is foolish in the world to shame the wise, God chose what is weak in the world to shame the strong, God chose what is low and despised in the world, even things that are considered nothing, to bring to naught things that are, so that no human being might boast in the presence of God" (I Cor 1:26-29). Power and splendor have no place in the kingdom of God.

Hence it follows what kind of soul-winning power lies in cultural works, in art, science, and technical progress. Christianity needs culture. No one has done more for it than the Church. But it would be a fatal mistake to believe that we can win souls for Christ with fine painting, brilliant scientific achievements, political power and impressive technological advancement. Anyone who reads the Gospels attentively knows that Christ did not reject these things, but that He won people to Himself not by means of any of this but purely through the holiness of His life, the beauty of His miracles and the convincing power of His word—in other words, through the power of the supernatural.

Christ hung on the cross. In fact, He always does. We would consider it an insult if anyone depicted Him as "the Man of Joy." We can see Him only as "the Man of Sorrows," with cross and sacrifice as His companions. Thus was wiped out all the sin and all the guilt which man had brought on himself and through which he forgot God and neighbor. Out of egotism. Redemption from egotism can happen only through its opposite. And the opposite of self-seeking is selflessness and disinterestedness. Selflessness at any price. Selflessness even to death on the cross. This is what Christ did. Absolute selflessness.

As Christ goes, so goes Christianity. It is well known how the world, especially in our time, is constantly accusing the Catholic Church of pursuing the struggle for its rights and for souls only for selfish purposes. The selfishness of political power and clerical domination. The selfishness of priestly adulation. The selfishness of worldly ease and comforts.

The Church of today possesses **only** one way of convincing modern mankind of its love. And that way is to mount the Cross of

Christ. To allow herself to be ridiculed. To move forward with absolute unselfishness, becoming poor like Christ, to do good and to pray for her enemies. Then she will experience a resurrection! The road to triumph for the Church leads by way of Golgotha, to the poor, humble, crucified Savior Jesus Christ.

CHRIST'S SUFFERINGS

AT THE GATEWAY OF LENT

If there were no Lent, it would have to be invented. It is not only a religious and moral necessity, but a psychological one. In the hustle and bustle of everyday life, there has to be a time to pause, breathe deeply and think. With everything and everyone relentlessly pushing and shoving, the devil, that old deceiver, lets soap bubbles loose in the air which people think are some sort of good luck charm. Then comes Ash Wednesday and the bubble of pleasure bursts with a resounding pall.

A process of unmasking has started in modern culture, something which Divine Providence has permitted since about 1914—a certain gradual disillusionment, even if it occurs here and there only to a minority. But the process of disillusionment—which can be the beginning of a healing process—is an undeniable fact, and thus provides the psychological foundation for understanding and experiencing the inner reality of Lent.

Lent is spiritual rest. When the first railroad was being built in Germany, the medical faculty of the University of Erlangen published an official warning to the effect that prospective passengers on the railroad would all suffer irreparable brain damage from moving at such high speeds. The learned gentlemen were mistaken. It would have been more correct to say that in the age of electricity and factories, telephone and radio, cinema and sports events, coffee and alcohol (everything, in other words, that tends to put nerves on end)—in such a world, if there were no churches, there would be ten times as many insane asylums. The Catholic Church, with its tabernacle and chapel of Our Lady, is the best nerve tonic around.

The world is excitement. God is peace. The house of God is an island of rest and quiet. Even on a purely natural level, the myste-

rious stillness of a Catholic church works wonders in calming, re-
laxing, strengthening, invigorating, healing. Think of Psalm 83:
"How lovely is thy dwelling place, O Lord of Hosts! My soul longs,
yea, faints for the courts of the Lord; my heart and flesh sing for joy
to the living God. Even the sparrow finds a home, and the swallow
a nest for herself, where she may lay her young: Thy altars, O Lord
of hosts, my King and my God. For a day in thy courts is better
than a thousand elsewhere." Harried, hassled, nerve-racked humanity, come and rest a while!

Lent is reflection. Reflection on what is most important. Most
urgent. Eternity. Man returns to himself once more. Of course he
does not belong to himself alone. He belongs to others: to his family, to his Church, to his country. And also, and above all, to himself
and to God. This creates another psychological need. To become
himself again, to put his head in his hands and think about what
has happened, what is now happening, and what is unavoidably going to happen. In the quiet hours of Lent man gets to know himself
again.

We are proud of our education. We have done much research.
Have we not gone all over the world on trips of exploration? But
don't we remain strangers to ourselves? We in the modern world
know how to add. Let us add up the debit and credit sides of our
soul. We love history. But what is the use of digging into the origins
and development of our country, if we do not understand the
meaning and direction of our own life? And what is the point of
running around the cities and villages, hills and rivers of our homeland, if we do not know our own interior geography? Get back to
yourself! The forty days of Lent should put you in touch with your
own personality.

Lent is a return to Christ. With so much attention given to personality development and careers, we have too little time for ourselves. We are like the fruit on the tree that is not quite ripe. What
is happening in the great, wide world must have a single meaning,
unless we want to say world history is a tissue of meaningless insanity. The deepest meaning must focus on Christ. Everything was created in Christ and for Christ, and in Him all things hold together
(Col. 1:16ff.). Lent, therefore, must concentrate on Christ. Human

renewal can only consist in everything going back to Christ as Head (*cf.* Eph. 1:10).

But Christ is the Crucified. So we have the theme for our coming Lenten reflections: the Christ Who sweated blood, Who was scourged, Who was crowned with thorns, Who carried His cross and was nailed to it. With St. Paul we say, "When I came to you, I did not come proclaiming to you the testimony of God in lofty words or wisdom. For I decided to know nothing among you except Jesus Christ and Him crucified. And I was with you in weakness and in much fear and trembling; and my speech and my message were not in plausible words of wisdom, but in demonstration of the Spirit and power, that your faith might not rest in the wisdom of men but in the power of God. Yet among the mature we do impart wisdom, although it is not a wisdom of this age or of the rulers of this age, who are doomed to pass away" (I Cor. 2:1 ff.).

Lent is conversion. This is not just a theory. Not even just a pious theory. It is not just a matter of talk, but of deep-seated transformation. The goal of Lent is the Resurrection. The new man. Thus says the Lord, "Return to me with all your heart, with fasting, with weeping, and with mourning; and rend your hearts and return to the Lord, your God, for he is gracious and merciful, slow to anger, and abounding in mercy, and repents of evil" (Joel 2:12ff.).

Lent is wringing our hands. Weeping, crying to heaven to God. The new world must come from heaven. It is a grace, and grace, in the usual order of things, is bound up with kneeling, folding our hands, and praying. We are proud of our gift of tongues. But of what use is it to speak all the languages of the earth, if we do not know how to talk to God? *Orate, fratres!* Pray, brethren! Above all, pray with the sacrifice of Christ which is taking place now. Holy Mass.

Thus we are at the gateway of Lent. By listening, praying, doing penance, we march on toward sanctity. We seek peace and rest. We will find what we seek. We will find what we have not found on the street, in nightclubs, in the bank, in fashion magazines—and never will. We shall find the key to paradise which Adam lost. And the key is the Cross. And there is no one to open the door except Christ—the Christ Who sweated blood and was crucified.

THE WORLD'S GUILT AND ITS ATONEMENT

A God and King Who sweats blood, is scourged and crowned with thorns, Who carries His Cross and is nailed to it, as St. Paul says, is a stumbling-block to the Jews and foolishness to the Gentiles. If the history of the passion shows us a God Who is bound with fetters and an Almighty Who is vulnerable, then we are faced with incomprehensible mysteries. The idea of a God of power would seem to have evaporated into a myth. Is it not damning evidence against a religion that its Founder should be abandoned, betrayed, rejected by the people and the authorities pour out His Blood on the scaffold?

Let's admit it: We are faced with a profound mystery. A God Who suffers seems an impossibility and a contradiction. A stumbling-block. Nonsense. Something against which right reason and all the finer feelings rise up in protest. But only apparently. Only superficially. Anyone who goes into divine revelation by the light of faith and steeps himself in this mystery, will find there the key to all questions. The passion of Our Lord, far from being foolishness, is the only answer for the mind and heart of man in the question of the world's guilt and how to atone for it—the problem of sin and punishment which has racked the best brains for thousands of years.

The world's guilt is a great, undeniable fact of world history. In the beginning God made heaven and earth. The masterpiece belongs to the Master. The creation belongs to the Creator. Man is no exception. Man is indeed king of the earth, God's representative and the irreplaceable king and proprietor. But only on the condition that he acknowledge he is the property and servant of God. Because man is from God, he must belong to God, and because he belongs to God, he must be at the service of God. Exclusively. Everywhere. Constantly. In every respect. To be man means to be created, and to be created means to do the Will of the Creator. To be man means to be radically, totally, permanently in submission to the absolute sovereignty of the Almighty. An unconditional, joyful eternal Yes of faith, of humility and of obedience. This has to be the real meaning of world history.

Then the unspeakable, the unfathomable happened. Adam, the king of the earth, said No to God for the first time. The No of unbelief, of pride and of disobedience. This was the revolution that became the pattern of every rebellion on earth since that time. Since that time the language of the sons of Adam has been a language of No. A million times No: No, we will not believe; No, we will not serve; No, we will not obey—day and night such cries rise up to heaven and earth. The great majority of mankind since Adam has been at war with God. This is the world's guilt. The world's guilt is the great, incontestable fact of world history.

Guilt must be paid for. The guilt of the world demands the punishment of the world. Because God is God, He must be holy. He must hate evil. Because God is God, He must be just. He must punish the wicked. Because God is God, there must be punishment by death. Because God is God, there must be a hell. Realizing these things has been the daily burden of mankind since the beginning. We go through life weighed down and bent over with guilt. We suspect, we know that somehow, somewhere, at some time there must be a reckoning. A judgment.

It is against this background that we must consider the Passion. It is in this light that we must situate the Christ Who sweats blood, is scourged and crowned with thorns, Who carries His Cross, and is nailed to it. Christ is God. Of course. But Christ is also a man. More than that. Christ is mankind. He is not merely a private individual—someone or another. He is in a certain sense ourselves. He is, as Adam once was, the absolute representative of mankind. He willingly takes upon Himself all the debts of the human race collectively. On every account payable, the Name of Jesus is there as co-signer, the sole responsible and the security. It is Jesus Who bears the world's guilt and the world's punishment.

Isaias sees Christ in this light. For him Christ is mankind. Mankind atoning for its sins. One Man for all men! As the prophet shows Him, He is scorned. The outcast of men. The man of sorrows. A countenance distorted with grief. An outcast. Smitten by God. Wounded for our sins. Bruised for our transgressions. He takes our sorrow on Himself. He bears all our ills. All our transgressions the Lord has laid on Him. And He opens not His mouth. Like a sheep that is led to the slaughter. Like a lamb that before its shearers is dumb. He is sacrificed. But only because He wanted to be! Christ, Who bears the sins and the punishment of the world (*cf.* Is. 53).

We must not lose sight of this truth when we consider the Way of the Cross or the sorrowful mysteries of the rosary. Christ in His agony on the Mount of Olives—this is ourselves. Mankind sweating blood. Christ at the pillar of the flagellation, this is ourselves. Mankind enduring flagellation. Christ, crowned with thorns and wearing the purple robe in mockery, this is ourselves. Mankind crowned with thorns. Christ carrying His Cross, this is ourselves. Mankind carrying its cross. Christ being crucified, this is ourselves. Mankind being crucified. The story of the passion is our story. The story of mankind.

The lesson we must draw from this is a deeper belief in the dogma of the unity and solidarity of mankind. That we are all organs of one body put together so as to form one single organism. This is not true, says Communism. It is not true, because we are a formless mass, without personality and without rights. Not true because we have no personal souls, no private lives, no individual duties, no personal future. The real truth is that, alongside our private lives, we have a life in society, alongside our individual duties, we have a collective duty; alongside our personal responsibility, we have a collective responsibility, a general responsibility. If man is human, then he must be by nature a member. Member of a family group. Member of a national group. Member of a religious group. Member of a majority group. And for this reason his fate is tied up with that of others.

And for this reason he experiences feelings, suffering and atonement along with others. As the Incarnation of Christ led inexorably to His passion (whoever says A must say B), so for us, being born in a certain country and at a certain time means we have a share in the passion, we have a duty to share in the suffering and in the atonement with our own people in our own time. The same is true of our re-birth. Whoever, in the waters of baptism, is grafted onto Christ and His Mystical Body, the Church, becomes bound up with the Head, Who sweated blood, was scourged and crowned with thorns, Who carried His Cross and was nailed upon it. And he must suffer and make atonement as a contribution to the faith of the group. There are those who are called to share in the passion in a special way as victims for sin. In a certain sense we all are. You cannot become a Christian without a share in the Crucifixion. "Whoever does not take up his cross and come after me, cannot be my disciple" (Lk. 14:27).

Years ago in Berlin, posters appeared all over town saying "Jesus Lives!" It was an invitation to a great protest rally against a prominent atheist. More than twenty thousand people showed up. Every time a speaker gave vent to his outrage at the way freethinkers were crucifying Christ in the modern world, every time he got carried away with enthusiasm and shouted "Jesus Lives," there was a roar of applause like thunder.

A newspaper reporter said that people returned to Christ in droves. It seems to me that a Christ Who is crucified and dies for His people is greater than a Christ Who lives and triumphs for His people. When is the time coming when mankind returns in droves to Christ *because* He is a Christ Who suffers and makes atonement, Who carries His Cross and is nailed upon it?

CHRIST IN A SWEAT OF BLOOD

It **is** Holy Thursday. Twelve men come down the hill from the Temple. It is Jesus and His apostles. Talking in hushed and solemn tones, they cross the Brook Kedron and climb the other side of the Mount of Olives. Steep cliffs and thick, dark clumps of trees project ghostly shapes into the moonlit night air. The twelve reach the Garden of Gethsemane. Jesus loves this quiet spot. Often He prayed here the whole night through. Far from the noise of the city.

Jesus is unspeakably sad. On all sides great clouds of terrible mental images press in upon Him. He begins to shudder and to shiver. "My soul," He says, "is sorrowful, even unto death." Then He separates Himself from the apostles and goes a stone's throw further on. Tradition has it that He goes into a nearby cave under an overhanging cliff. He is like one seeking shelter from a terrible storm.

Christ makes an examination of conscience. And Christ, as we have seen, is mankind. Christ is here preparing His general confession for Easter, which He will make on Good Friday on Golgotha in the name of all mankind. And this examination of conscience is threefold: a look into the world of sin, a look at the passion, and a look at the atonement for sin to come.

Christ's look into the world of sin. What Christ is doing is making the examination of conscience of One Who is omniscient. Before His eyes flow the sins of all nations, all ages, all men. A veritable flood of sin. A vast ocean of evil and wretchedness, of godlessness and immorality, of hatred and murder, of deceit and injustice, of materialism and sensuality, of ingratitude and cowardice. Hell. The history of the world is a history of devils and beasts, of murders and thefts. Dripping with blood, reeking of corruption. Crying out to heaven.

We speak of a *mysterium iniquitatis.* The mystery of evil. Sin, considered quantitatively and qualitatively. No one has ever seen so deeply into the mystery of evil as Christ in His examination of conscience on the Mount of Olives. And we can understand how the German mystic, Anna Catherine Emmerich, in depicting this *mysterium iniquitatis* pressing down upon Christ, can speak of the most dreadful, shocking, terrifying images.

Christ is a man. Nothing weak or feeble about Him. He is the *Ischyros,* the Man of Strength, as the Good Friday liturgy calls Him. But now, as He sees before Him the complete and intrinsic hideousness and godlessness of sin in countless images, He shudders and bows down and falls to the ground, covered by a profuse sweat. Sin is to Him incomprehensible, horrible, evil, ghastly. Our examinations of conscience are often so mechanical. A superficial string of thoughts. Christ on the Mount of Olives shows us how we should not just count our sins in examining our conscience, but weigh, ponder them. As horrible. As frightful. As God-denying.

Christ looks at His passion. We can and should in our examination of conscience consider sin not only in itself but as the denial of God in the world. It is also man's worst enemy. Suicidal. As every divine law contributes to our well-being and health and growth, so every violation, sooner or later, visibly or invisibly, means corruption and destruction. Violation of and emancipation from God's commandment carries its own punishment in itself—with relentless logical and merciless justice.

Thus in His examination of conscience Christ, in His bloody sweat, immediately after the panorama of the sin of the world, sees the panorama of His passion. Jesus sees before His eyes the betrayal of Judas, the flight of the disciples, His condemnation by the High Priest, Peter's denial, the judgment of Pilate, the mockery, the flagellation, the carrying of the Cross and the horrible hammering of the nails, the sneers of the Pharisees, the piercing of His side. And this forces a sweat of blood through His pores.

This should be our model for examination of conscience. Reflecting on sin should lead us to reflect on its consequences. To reflect on what follows after. What must follow. Like the fruit from the seed. The consequences of our sins. For body and soul. For ourselves and others. For the present and for the future. For time and eternity. Every sin has a complete passion story behind it. Only when the awareness of this passion history has sunk into one's consciousness can one say that he understands sin.

Christ looks into the world of future suffering and atonement. The Christ Who sweats blood on the Mount of Olives is entirely alone in His unspeakable anguish and yet right in the midst of a multitude of souls. He sees in spirit all the future sufferings of His apostles, disciples and His friends. All the tribulations and persecutions of His Church until the end of time. Christ in His bloody sweat is also an on-going Christ. Gethsemane is not just a part of history, but a part of the on-going present. We can even say Christ in His bloody sweat is ourselves, and all mankind today. We can also say the Church of today, sweating blood and in fear of death, is Christ.

If we do not know this, then we do not know the Church—or know it only superficially. The blood of Gethsemane and Golgotha must flow uninterruptedly if the world is not to collapse. It flows in an invisible stream in the Holy Sacrifice of the Mass. But it flows also in a visible stream in the sacrifice of the suffering Church. As Paul said to the Colossians, "I rejoice in my sufferings for your sake, and in my flesh I complete what is lacking in Christ's afflictions for the sake of his body, that is, the Church" (1:24).

The stigmata of St. Francis and hundreds of others, in spite of their obviously miraculous nature, are in a certain way perfectly understandable. I would be more surprised if there were no stigmatics in the Church than I would be to hear of new blood in the Mystical Body of the Church. For the Church in its bloody sweat is part of Christ in His bloody sweat. The sufferings of the Lord, says Pope St. Leo, must go on until the end of the world.

Herein lies the explanation of the divinity and truth of the Catholic Church. I believe in the Catholic Church not only because I believe in the Gospel—and the Gospel, I am convinced, is Catholic. I believe in the Catholic Church not only because it goes back to the time of the apostles and extends to the ends of the earth. I believe in the Catholic Church not only because miracles bear witness to it.

I believe in the Catholic Church also because she is the Church that sweats blood, is scourged and crowned with thorns, carries her cross and is nailed upon it and thus must be the Bride of Christ Who sweats blood, is scourged and crowned with thorns, carries His Cross and is nailed upon it. If it is true that the Western world is headed for a fresh persecution of Christians, then there will be fresh martyrs to show that this must be the true Church, for whom not only do the greatest minds write the finest books, but also for whom the noblest spirits joyfully and repeatedly shed their blood.

CHRIST AT THE PILLAR

I think there is nothing in the history of the passion, including the crucifixion, so horrible, gruesome and barbaric as the scourging. Anna Catherine Emmerich depicts it in lurid colors. A couple of executioner's henchmen, hardened criminals, more devil than human, stretch the disrobed body of Our Lord tightly to a freestanding pillar in the marketplace. The ghastly process of flagellation lasted some three quarters of an hour.

The first scourging took place with rods of tough fiber. With savage blows the two barbarians whipped the back of the Savior, writhing under the blows like a worm being crushed. Then two other hangman's knaves took over with a savage beating inflicted with a kind of thorny vine, making the blood spurt out in all directions. The third pair of torturers beat Jesus with thongs which had iron hooks fastened to the ends, so that whole pieces of skin and flesh were torn from the ribs. A frightening picture of misery, this Christ of the flagellation.

But Christ at the pillar, as we said, is all mankind. If the passion is considered as Jesus doing vicarious atonement for the benefit of the whole human race, then this scene cannot fail to make its impact. There can be no passion without the flagellation of the body, because there is no guilt of the world without the guilt of the flesh. Man is twofold. Soul and body. He is twofold, because He is the midpoint of creation, the link between the spiritual world and the material world. Between angel and animal. The upward connection is through the soul of man, the downward through his body.

Man's fate is dependent on whether it draws him upward or downward, whether his center of gravity is in the spirit or in the flesh. Whether he wants to become spirit or become animal—these are the two opposing tendencies in history. Toward God or beast. Here we have the Either-Or, before which every man in this life stands. We must choose between these two, between the tendency to divinization, which subordinates the flesh to the spirit, and the tendency to the animal, which subordinates the spirit to the flesh.

With original sin in the Garden of Eden the downward tendency starts in mankind, and this bestializing process, as the spiritual writers point out, is symbolized in a threefold catastrophe. The first catastrophe is Noah's Flood and the destruction of the antediluvian world. What caused this engulfing, in which all mankind perished with the exception of eight persons? He Whose hand broke the dike and let in the sea and opened the sluices of heaven, tells us in three words: Man became flesh (Gen. 6:6). The flood of water was the result of the flood of sin.

A second catastrophe was the destruction of the pagan Roman world. Man had quickly forgotten the lesson learned in the days of Noah. Paganism had over-run the world and with paganism came again a wave of sensualism. Sensuality. Sensuality was not only in command, it became a veritable religion. The flesh became a god. Money, dinner parties, baths, theaters, even the temple served their lust for pleasure. Rome, which had conquered the world, was conquered by the flesh. The Rome of the Caesars became a putrid carcass. And so the word of Scripture was fulfilled: Where the carcass is, there the eagles will gather. The northern eagle of the barbarian tribes fed on the carcass of Rome. The almighty Roman Empire was engulfed by a new flood of punishment for sin. But a deluge of blood. Because it had become flesh!

Then we meet a third Noah's Flood, *i.e.*, the third catastrophe of the flesh. The world of the end times, as the Apocalypse says, will be like the world of Noah. More than a slave of the beast ever did, it gave itself with unprecedented shamelessness to all manner of sordidness. Man again becomes flesh. But God has had enough. A third flood to wipe out sin, the flood of fire, will put an end to the world-become-flesh.

In the midst of this world-become-flesh we situate now the pillar with the Christ of the flagellation. Let us not forget: the Christ Who is bound to the pillar and scourged is mankind atoning for its sensuality. The pillar is a tombstone and also a monument. A tombstone for the flesh which has been mastered by the new man of the spirit. As St. Paul says in the Epistle to the Romans concerning the city-become-flesh: "We know that our old self was crucified with him so that the sinful body might be destroyed, and we might no longer be enslaved to sin" (6:6). "So then, brethren, we are debtors, not to the flesh to live according to the flesh..." (8:12). The pillar has become a monument to the liberation of the spirit from the tyranny of the flesh. A freedom column.

Human speech uses the same word for two different and opposing forces. We call the suffering and death of Our Lord His Passion. We also call "passion" the concupiscence in man that is a result of original sin. Passion is overcome by the Passion, the suffering of sin-laden mankind through the suffering of the God-Man. We build up the strength to overcome in the fight against sensuality of the body from the streams of blood from the flagellated body of Christ.

The problem of chastity and purity of the body depends essentially on the body of Our Lord, Who sweated blood, was crowned with thorns and scourged, Who carried His Cross and was nailed to it. The body of man, poisoned by concupiscence, must be detoxified and renewed through the Holy Eucharist, which is the Body of the Lord under the appearance of bread. Holy Communion. The problem of chastity is essentially a Eucharistic problem. It is solved at the table of the Lord—not exclusively, but primarily so. Through the monthly Communion, the Sunday Communion, the frequent Communion, early Communion. The paganized body must, through Holy Communion, become Christian again.

Yet we cannot be content with Communion, with relying on the flagellated Body of Christ. Whoever takes the flagellated Christ to himself, must also take the spirit of sacrifice. We talk about the fitness of the human body, and we think we can maintain a strong, healthy body by means of exercise and sports. The rehabilitation and fitness of the human body is, in the first place, a moral and ascetical matter. What the older generation called penance.

A life of regularity, simplicity, modesty, early rising. The body must again become the servant in the house and not the master. This is the meaning of the Church's forty days of Lent, which is more important for the health of modern man than sports and weightloss programs.

It is a matter of life and death. We are going by leaps and bounds to that time of the fall of Rome, when life could be summed up in two words: *panem et circenses!* Bread and circuses! Food and entertainment! Life today is pouring itself out in sensual pleasures. But a nation which feeds on pleasures and thirsts only for pleasures, gets out of control. The fattened slave breaks loose. If he succeeds in throwing off his chains, he will break them over the head of his tormentor. Then follows crime upon crime, catastrophe upon catastrophe, until finally the collapse. We must get mankind back to the pillar of the flagellation, so as to learn the wisdom of the Christ Who was so savagely beaten.

CHRIST CROWNED WITH THORNS

After the scourging the governor's men took Jesus and led Him to the courtyard of the house of judgment and surrounded the house with a battalion of soldiers. The executioners' henchmen tore off Jesus' clothes, threw on Him an old, torn, scarlet military cloak and pushed Him down on the nearest chair. They plaited a crown of thorn vines and set it on Jesus' head. And they put a reed in His right hand. All this they did with a mock festive air, as if they were crowning a real king. Then they came up to Him, bowed and knelt before Him and in great derision cried, "Hail, King of the Jews!"

They spit on Him, took the reed and struck Him on the head and on the back. This was a mockery of the then customary ceremony of coronation, but with the most horrible perversion and terrible abusiveness. An enthronement planned in hell and carried out with hatred and scorn for the Divine Heart of Jesus.

Well, Christians, what do you say to this? How do you like this picture of Christ? A Head covered with blood and wounds. Pain topped off with ridicule. The Divine Head surrounded with a crown of thorns. We read in history the story of a conversion. A certain saint brought a frivolous, light-headed friend of his to conversion in an unusual way. He sat at his window in such a way that all the neighbors could see him looking with great interest at something like a mirror. The friend took an interest in the "mirror" and wanted one for himself. He got his wish. He was given one of these wonderful "mirrors." It was a picture of Christ crowned with thorns. The "mirror" was the occasion of the conversion. I wish I could give everyone today just such a "mirror."

We call ourselves Christians, reflections of Christ. To be a Christian means to be a painter. We have the task of painting a copy of Jesus Christ directly from the original, which has been given to us as model and guide. The copyist must study his original carefully—every angle of the face, every line, every shade of color. After a close study of the original, he must reproduce it, angle for angle, line for line, stroke for stroke, until you could write on the copy the words *concordat cum originali*—it agrees with the original. A Christian's head must be the head of Christ, a Christian face must be the face of Christ, every line just as in the original. The particular judgment consists in determining how close the copy comes to the original, then in sending the true copies into the picture gallery of heaven, the imperfect likenesses to purgatory for corrections, with those bearing no likeness to the model discarded in eternal fire.

It is part of the business of Lent to check how far we have strayed from our model in copying the picture of Christ. After a great victory over the Parthians, the Emperor Septimius Severus returned with his army to Rome and celebrated with a splendid procession. He gave the command that every soldier was to put a garland of flowers on his head and enter the city with that embellishment. One of the soldiers could not see his way clear to doing that. His garland he carried in his hand, not on his head. When questioned, he gave this beautiful answer: "I am a Christian. It is not right that a Christian should wear a crown of flowers, when Christ wore a crown of thorns and bled from a thousand wounds." The man's explanation was deemed unacceptable. He was dismissed from the army and thrown in prison. This gave the learned Tertullian the opportunity to write a defense of this soldier. He put together a book on the custom of bestowing garlands on festive occasions and thought such a crown a poor comparison with Christ's crown of thorns. It is not seemly that a Christian should wear a crown of flowers. The head of a Christian should be like the head of Christ!

The head of modern man must from now on resemble the Head crowned with thorns. Your head is empty! You want to be beautiful. All the latest fashions and new cosmetics you have to have, to draw the attention of your contemporaries. Your ideal is to be seen, to be the object of talk and admiration—or at least envy. St. Paul said, "I desire...that women should adorn themselves modestly and sensibly in seemly apparel, not with carefully dressed hair, gold, pearls or costly attire" (I Tim. 2:9). People seem not to take notice of such admonitions any more. Spring is coming. Especially in the women's world there is great fussing over new fashions. The terrible seriousness of our times should inspire the greatest simplicity and modesty in clothing. Unfortunately there is no evidence that we have learned a lesson in the school of plain, beautiful simplicity. The question of new clothes is part of the preparation for Lent. It must be answered in front of the "mirror" of the Head covered with blood and wounds. The Christian conscience should contribute a word at this point. To the question, How close do you come to the original—the Head crowned with thorns, all serious Christians should be able to answer: This is a head of Christ. It is a perfect copy of the original!

What about the facial lines of modern man? How does the eye look? The mouth? We all have nerves. We are all weak, fragile people. We get jittery, irritated, moody, depressed. All this shows up on the face. And is reflected like a photograph. You go to confession and say, "What am *I* going to do? I am so upset that I hardly know what I am saying or doing." A suggestion. Take your "pocket mirror" in your hand—the picture of Christ crowned with thorns. Compare the copy with the original! You might be ashamed of yourself! You might lower your eyes. You might weep and strike your breast over the dissimilarity. The original is a picture of heavenly peace surrounded by a raging storm of persecution and ridicule. The original does not show anger blazing out of the eyes. Or gnashing of the teeth. No cursing or complaining. The original breathes a marvelous gentleness, humility, love, patience. One who curses, screams, hates, gets nervous and impatient, is no head of Christ. Get busy, painter, you must do better than that!

The head of a Christian should be like the Head of Christ not only externally, but above all internally. If the inside of modern man's head could be photographed, what would it look like? Like an anthill. Like a heaving sea. Like a field of slaughter. Like a storm-filled sky. Like darkest night. Modern man's head so often harbors doubt, an uncatholic spirit of criticism, disbelief. The modern brain, so often even in those who want to be good Catholics, is poisoned with the germs of error, with Protestant, Liberal, Socialist, Modernist ideas, gleaned from the daily newspapers and from talk. The head of a Christian, like the Head of Christ, must bow humbly before every word that comes from the mouth of God. The Christian head accepts in childlike faith the authority of the Church founded by Christ. The head of the Christian is like the ripe grain which bows down in gratitude before its Creator. Not like the cut stalk, which sticks up proudly, stiffly and independently. When you are preparing your Easter Confession, look also at what is inside. Check your thoughts. Are they favorably inclined to the one Holy Roman Catholic and Apostolic Church? Toward priests? Like the original? Like Jesus?

We can push the comparison between original and copy still further. We can look into the difference between the Christ Who prayed, thirsted and bled, and the Christian who is bored and tired of praying and who seeks his own pleasure. Everyone can make this comparison by himself at home in the quiet of his own heart, in the spirit of the words of St. Paul: "Those whom God foreknew he also predestined to be conformed to the image of his Son, in order that he might be the first-born among many brethren" (Rom. 8:29). Painter, paint on. Painter, paint better. Paint with the colors of the

Gospels and the saints. It is not a matter of indifference. Eternity depends on it. Painter, paint like a Christian!

THE WAY OF THE CROSS

An old legend has it that St. Peter, in the year 67 AD, during the reign of the Emperor Nero, at first tried to escape a martyr's death by running away. On the outskirts of Rome, where there is now a little commemorative chapel, he saw—according to the legend—the Lord carrying His Cross. *Domine, quo vadis?*—Where are you going, Lord? asked Peter. "I'm going to die for you once more," was the answer. Peter understood the subtle suggestion of cowardice implied in these words of the Lord. He turned around and went back and on June 29 he was crucified. If chapels were built on every spot where someone tried to run away from his cross, the highways, hills and valleys would be dotted with them. We are quite willing to hear the story of Jesus Who bore the guilt of the world and Who paid the guilt of the world and the infinite satisfaction that He accomplished. But we fall willingly into the error of Protestantism if we think that faith in the Redemption achieved by Our Savior is in itself enough to save us.

We see how Christ—Who called Himself the Way—left His bloody footprints on the road to eternal life. We are not happy to walk this painful high road, least of all when it leads over the Mount of Olives and Mount Calvary. We much prefer to go with the crowd on the low road. With the majority. But it is not the Christianity of the low road that leads to heaven, but rather the Christianity of the sacrificial way. Christians must walk **in** the footsteps of Christ. Christians must become followers of the Christ Who bore His cross.

We now consider the Redeemer and His Cross—this is the heart and soul of Christianity. It is the unconditional submission to the Will of God—in the form of patience and obedience. All the sin and all the evil of the world has a single cause: transgression of the Divine Will. All sanctity in the world, all redemption knows one rule only: return to the Will of the Father.

When He came into the world—as St. Paul, enlightened by the Holy Ghost, tells us—Christ said, "Sacrifices and offerings thou

hast not desired, but a body hast thou prepared for me; in burnt offerings and sin offerings thou hast taken no pleasure. Then I said,
Lo, I have come to do thy will, O God, as it is written of me in the
roll of the book" (Heb. 10:5ff.).

The fundamental thought of Jesus' life, His prayer, morning
and evening, His whole life, is: *Ecce venio—Behold, I come.* Lord
God, do what Thou willst. Here I am!

Now His suffering assumes monstrous proportions before His
eyes. His human nature shrinks from the agony which He is to endure in body and soul for all mankind. He prays—as was His human right—to be spared. "My Father, to Thee all things are
possible: take this chalice from Me! Yet not My Will but Thine be
done!" No sufferer ever felt a greater desire for relief than Christ on
this occasion. He asked to be spared this horrible and agonizing
death. And yet even this thought was of secondary importance. He
had another thought with which the whole fabric of His being was
interwoven: the Will of His Father! And if His affliction is as great
as the ocean—what does that matter? And if all the evil of hell is
unleashed like a hurricane over His innocent Head—so be it! And
if the most justifiable wish and the most humble prayer goes unan-
swered—well, only one thing is of any importance in heaven and
on earth: the Will of the Father!

Jesus recognizes one all-important fact: There is a central point
around which everything in the world revolves: God. And this God
can do what He wills, and what He does is good. It is easy for us to
believe in an almighty, all-loving and all-knowing God when this
almighty, all-knowing and all-loving God does what pleases us. But
it is hard in times of suffering and contradiction to believe in such
a God. But God is God, whether we see Him as Father or Lord or
Lawgiver or Judge. In every case it means only one thing for us:
God's Will as the law of the world! This is the lesson of the Redeemer carrying His cross. We are entitled to try to escape from evil. We
are entitled to use all natural and supernatural means to avoid the
cross. We are entitled to talk about our pains as much as we like.
But we are not entitled to rise up in rebellion. We have no right to
complain about God. God must have the last word.

The last word must always be the word of resignation and patience, an unconditional submission to Divine Providence. The *ecce*

venio: behold, I come; do what Thou willst. Lord God, here I am. The rights of God rank higher than the rights of man. The only thing needful is that God must always be God! God must always be right. Because God's decisions are decisions of wisdom, of justice and of love! Here lies the secret of patience. The fundamental thought of the suffering of Jesus and of the Christian is the same: the Father's Will—that alone!

The other thought: Unconditional submission of man to the Divine Will is the secret of obedience! Just as the stars in the sky above do not meander around freely, but follow prescribed paths; just as when a house is in process of being built, stone is laid upon stone not just any old way, but following exactly the plans handed down from architect to builder, so also the life of man, as the greatest of all works of art, cannot be left to whim. It must be worked out according to the design of the Master Architect and carried through to its completion. Working it out is a matter of grace and free will, but the plan is God's. So too in the life of Jesus—His place of birth, His Mother, His youth, His field of activity, His passion, where He died—all this was determined from all eternity. And what did the Savior have His eye on, from Bethlehem all the way to Golgotha? He, the Perfect Man—as even unbelievers call Him— has only one concern: to fulfill His life work according to the plans of the Father for His life.

As Jesus sat at Jacob's well, tired and hungry at midday, and His disciples brought food from the nearby town of Sichar, they said to Him, "Master, eat!" But He said to them, "I have food to eat that you know not. My food is to do the will of him who sent me, and to complete his work." And on the last night of His life He exclaimed, "Father, I have gloried thee on earth. I have completed the work thou gavest me to do." The life of this greatest of all men is an unconditional submission to the Will of His Father. Obedience. A work that follows the life plans down to the tiniest detail.

In our time an unrestrained freedom and license amounting almost to drunkenness and insanity prevails. In such an atmosphere there is no truth more urgently necessary than this: Life must be lived according to the eternal and unalterable plans of the Almighty! It is up to us to work out the ways and means, but the plan is God's. We can preach and write about freedom as much as we please. That is just what I am doing right here. But independence of the Will of God, Who lays down the law and guides us in it, is an idea of man who has lost not only his faith and his conscience but also his mind. You can rant and rave and carry on like a madman, but the ordinances of God you cannot change. You may plant, but every plant which the Father does not plant will be pulled up. You may build, but if the Lord does not build the house, then the builders are working in vain. There is only one thing to do: do like Jesus. Do the Father's Will.

Thousands of people are disappointed every day in their choice of a profession which decides the course of their lives, because they take as their guide not God and His eternal truths, but whim and passion. They do not turn to God in fervent prayer saying with St. Paul, "Lord, what wouldst thou have me do?" Millions go through life dissatisfied, their existence a waste of time because they want what they should not, and do not want what they should. People in the wrong place. Happiness and satisfaction do not depend on whether you have more or less health, popularity, money and less of the cross. The main thing is to know that you are standing in the right spot. In the place where God put you. To do your duty and to hold on until the Great Taskmaster transfers you. The will of man is his hell. The Will of God is man's heaven. The greatest comfort at death is to be able to say with Jesus, "Father, I have finished the work thou gavest me to do." The secret of my life was an unconditional surrender to the Father's Will—obedience.

It is not the Christianity of the broad way that leads to heaven, but rather the Christianity of the sacrificial way, the high road of patience and obedience. So our decision today must be: *Ecce venio—I come!* My resolution: to follow Jesus! Someone once asked Jesus, "Lord, are they few who will be saved?" He said to them, "Take care that you go in by the narrow gate; for I say to you, many will try to go in and not be able. If the master of the house has gone in and shut the doors, then they will stand outside, knock on the door and say, 'Lord, open to us!' And he will answer, 'I know you not. Whence are you?' Then they will begin to say, 'You taught in our streets.' And He will say to them, 'I know you not. Whence are you? Depart from me, ye evil-doers'" (Lk. 13:24ff.).

Let us therefore go in through the narrow gate. For high is the gate and wide the path that leads to damnation, and many there are who go that way. How narrow is the gate and how straitened the way that leads to life and how few there are who find it. The way to heaven is the high way, the way of sacrifice, the way of patience and obedience. *Ecce venio.* Behold, O Lord, I come.

THE TRIUMPH OF THE CRUCIFIED

We have lived Christ's Passion with Him. From one horror to the next. The agony in the garden, the scourging, the crowning with thorns, the way of the cross and Calvary are, humanly speaking, stages of a soul lost beyond redemption. All that can be said in the end is, *Consummatum est!* It's all over. Hopelessly ruined. Forever. And yet it turned out quite differently. The facts contradict the appearances. And the fact that outshines all other facts is the fact called Easter. The Resurrection of the Crucified. Jesus lives! Jesus triumphs! Jesus reigns!

We must now penetrate to the very heart of this fact. "If Christ is not risen, then," says St. Paul, "our preaching is vain and your faith is vain" (I Cor. 15:14). Christianity rises or falls with the fact of Easter. Christianity has a whole warehouse full of proofs to support its truth and its divine origin. But in an age when despair, empty-headedness and indifference are the rule, proofs have little value. With a butcher knife in one hand and a fire extinguisher in the other, the spirit of the modern world takes a contemptuous and sneering attitude toward the most convincing proofs.

What we need are facts which in their monumentality are as undeniable and incontrovertible as a mountain range dropped down in the world and before which all argument must bow. Facts which, insistent as the rays of the sun, demand to be accepted, not after lengthy investigation or scholarly explanation, but only with open eyes. You come, you see, you believe. Or you give up the right to be called a thinking person.

Such a fact that cannot be ignored because of its sheer monumentality is the victory of the Crucified, and not only the unique historical victory of Easter Day but also the on-going victory of the Crucified through the history of Christianity. Because Christianity is only the on-going life and on-going victory of Christ. The history of the Church is only the prolongation of Easter until the fullness of Easter at the end of the world. The nineteen hundred-year-old undeniable world-fact and the incomprehensible mystery consists of this, that a Jew, and a crucified Jew at that, stands as the midpoint of the world and is the object of the faith, hope, love, adoration and obedience of a good part of mankind.

There is a three-fold truth in that sentence. The first: the Jew, and a crucified Jew. The second: the midpoint. The third: the world. Let us dwell a moment on each of these three points. First of all there is the fact of a Jew. What is a Jew? At the time Jesus of Nazareth appeared, the Jew was the laughingstock of the world. The very name Jew, was synonymous with contemptibility, rejection and dishonor. It has remained so throughout all the centuries of Christian history—whether rightly or wrongly, I make no judgment, only the observation. The Jew was beneath contempt. Then comes the fact that Christ was a crucified Jew. At the time He suffered His crucifixion, it was the most shameful of penalties, the punishment of slaves, thieves, murderers, and political agitators.

The second fact in question is the central position of Christ in the spiritual life. Christ is not like any other. Not even like the great men who arise in every century, but rather as unique in twenty centuries. As teacher and shepherd of all people. As King of Kings and Lord of Lords. Even that is saying too little. As the Almighty. As the Adorable. As the hope of the human race. As the One Who, as no other ever did, loved with an intensity unto the shedding of His Blood. In other words, as the spiritual center of the last nineteen hundred years. And indeed such a center that even those who no longer have the courage to live by His laws, must still date every letter, every bill they send, every legal document they draw up, according to the fact of the birth of Christ!

The third point: the world. I mean the developed and civilized world. That world which for two thousand years has been the fruitful source of great genius and talent, of learning and art of so many nations. I mean the world without distinction of color, race or tongue. The world in the universal meaning of the word, the world of space and time. There was never a man so close to all mankind, so much a father and brother, so much one of themselves as Christ.

This is the great, monumental fact of the history of the world in its three incomprehensible mysteries: Christ Crucified, the King of the Jews, in the center of the world! This is His victory, a victory such that the world never saw its equal.

There is no effect without a cause. A fact of such monumental, overwhelming proportions must have a cause of superhuman and supernatural dimensions. It would be lunacy and a denial of all sound reason to assume that this nineteen hundred-year-old fact called Christianity simply appeared without a cause. And (what comes to the same thing) to assume that a mere man, and a Jew at that, and a condemned criminal, carries the entire Christian world on His shoulders, would be as ridiculous as the old pagan myth of the giant Atlas bearing up the earth and the heavens. It would be an effect without a cause. And belief in such a non-fact would be nonsense.

The great, incomparable and on-going fact of Easter, the Resurrection and the triumph of the Crucified through the centuries admits of only one explanation: the Crucified must be more than man. He must be Almighty. He must be God. Only the divinity of Christ answers the demands of reason, which demands a right relation between effect and cause. Divinely great effects demand a divinely great cause. The nineteen hundred years of Christianity, which struggled and prevailed over Judaism and paganism, against ridicule and rejection, against naked power and persecution—this is the work of a divine greatness. Christ the Crucified must have been sent by God.

Our answer to the Easter-event and the Easter-experience can only be a loud enthusiastic, joyful, hopeful Credo. The famous composer Joseph Haydn was a practicing Catholic and openly expressed his faith everywhere. One day one of his students was performing for him a Mass he had composed. The younger musician had set the Credo very softly and was playing it accordingly. The maestro listened a while, then became restless. His face reddened with indignation. Finally he blurted out to the startled young man: "Look here, how can you play the Credo like that? Don't you want to proclaim your faith loud and clear?"

This is the general mistake of the modern Catholic. He sings his Credo too softly. He is too shy, as if he did not have the benefit of infallible truth. As if he did not have the right—as in the Apocalypse—to sing Alleluias on the street. Today we must sing the Catholic Credo with gusto. Christ lives! Christ triumphs! Christ reigns!

CHRIST THE KING

PREFACE

We have not done our duty up to now. The present situation of the world, as has been said in our times, "must perhaps be blamed on the indifference and fearfulness of the good, who either avoid the fight or only put up weak resistance. That makes the enemy all the more impertinent and audacious."

Contemporary Catholicism is generally cautious and shy. They call that clever. In fact it is cowardly. Many of those who ought to be carrying "the torch of truth" forward with apostolic fervor instead hide it under a bushel basket. As Pius X once said, they treat the truth "like smugglers on the border," carrying Catholic fundamentals shyly hidden under their coats. They want to help with the reconstruction of Jerusalem, but they fearfully hide their little building stone in their pockets.

That must change. "The more one passes over the sweetest name of our Savior with abominable silence in the international conferences and the parliaments, the more necessary it is to cry it out all the louder and to proclaim everywhere the rights of His kingly power and dignity!" As though driven by Godly inspiration, we shall "bring Christ from out of the stillness and the hiddenness of the churches and carry Him through the streets of the cities, Christ Who came into the world, Whom the godless do not want to recognize, and restore to Him all His royal prerogatives." Christ must triumph and reign!

Long live Jesus the King!

Rev. Fr. Robert Mäder

TRANSLATOR'S FOREWORD

The direct inspiration for the series of articles that make up this part of the book* was Pope Pius XI's encyclical *Quas Primas*, instituting the Feast of Christ the King. However, for his political thought Fr. Mäder relied heavily on the great and astoundingly prophetic political philosopher and statesman, the Spaniard Don Juan Donoso Cortés, Marquis de Valdegama (1809-1853), who is practically unknown to the general public in America, but was one of the pioneering fighters for Catholicism against revolution and Liberalism. Fr. Mäder quotes or paraphrases Donoso Cortés a number of times in the following work, mainly the latter's two most famous speeches, "On Dictatorship" and "On Europe" (edited, translated and commented by Simona Draghici, Washington, D.C. 1989), but also his essay on *Catholicism, Liberalism and Order* (of no newer edition has appeared than that of J. C. Reville, New York/London, 1925).

Occasionally Fr. Mäder quotes his "favorite enemy," Friedrich Nietzsche, to whose philosophy he was of course passionately opposed, without mentioning his source. Because of time limitations, the translator did not search out the English versions of Nietzsche and Donoso Cortés and give exact source references.

All Biblical quotations are according to the Douay-Rheims version.

Dr. Eileen Kunze

---

* The articles in this book first appeared in the weekly magazine *Das Neue Volk* in the years 1926 and 1934.

THE KING OF THE CENTURIES

The world is a book. Every creature is a sentence in it. The Author and Publisher is the Triune God, with the co-operation of the angels and the human beings. It is the task of human intelligence to read God's thoughts from this book.

Every book has its basic theme, its dominant idea, its soul, a word that says everything, because it contains everything. The word that represents theme and content of the entire creation and the history of the world is called Jesus the King.

One can only understand this completely when the book has been read to the end and one can look back. Only Judgment Day, the final chapter of the book, will bring complete clarity as to the meaning of creation. Only when the Sign of the Son of Man appears in the heavens, when the lightning flashes from the beginning to the end, shall we understand the mysterious why and wherefore of all that happens in Jesus, the Alpha and Omega, the Beginning and the End, the immortal King of the centuries.

When the Sign of the Son of Man does not shine in heaven, then the world is robbed of its Light. Sun, moon and stars are of no use. One sees nothing, one understands nothing. One stumbles about in the dark and trips on all the paths. It is like a spiritual eclipse of the sun over the universe.

St. John painted for us the image of the eclipse of the sun as the great fact of the world without Christ in masterful strokes. Through Jesus, the Word, "all things were made...and without him was made nothing that was made. In him was life, and the life was the light of men. And the light shineth in darkness, and the darkness did not comprehend it" (Jn. 1:3-5).

Certainly the spiritual eclipse applies to the time before Jesus. Yet despite two thousand years of Christianity, it exists still today for a great part of Christendom. The words of St. John the Baptist are still valid: "...there hath stood one in the midst of you, whom you know not" (Jn. 1:26).

Jesus is by no means so well-known and loved as one ought to expect after nineteen centuries. Oh yes, they preach and talk and write a great deal about religious problems in our days. But the central Truth of our Religion: Jesus the Redemption of the world, the

Life of the souls and the nations, the Head and Heart of society, Jesus the King, is perceived in the immense, general, exclusively saving implications of that Truth only barely and only by a few.

The Sign of the Son of Man indeed can still be found in the churches, in the homes of Christian families, in the cemeteries and on the breasts of a few pious souls. However, it is not, as it once was, the sun that lights the day, that directs and influences all of public life, the thoughts and works of people. We are living in a period of spiritual night, cold, Christ-less night.

This ignorance is a world disaster. For it is always a precursor of serious catastrophes when the leaders of the peoples have become so blind that they cannot distinguish between day and night, true and false, the path and the chasm. Even worse than blindness, not being able to see, is not wanting to see anymore.

Right now this is the state of a large part of the human race. Whatever name it may carry, whether liberalism, neutrality, non-denominationalism or laicism, the sin of the modern world is that it does not want to see the Sign of the Son of Man in the heavens anymore.

Jesus is no longer recognized as public, commanding, life-giving Power. According to the valid constitutions, He has officially nothing more to say in the parliaments, in the halls of the ministries, in the courts, in the schools and in the workshops. At most His participation in the discussion is occasionally tolerated.

If one knows Who Jesus is: the Creator, the Conserver, the Savior, the Owner of earth, then one must regard the liberal sin, that of fundamental social refusal to recognize the spiritual monarchy of Christ over society, as the most grievous sin committed since Good Friday. It is deicide, God-murder, committed in the name of the law and of Satan, true Antichristianity. Cardinal Mercier therefore rightly called the official apostasy of the nations the greatest crime of our times.

At present this is the situation of the Sign of the Son of Man. They do not want it to shine in the heavens. Just like back then on Good Friday: We will not have Him reign over us!

But someday it will be otherwise. The world will not remain liberal forever. The artificial stars of earthly dimensions that want to eclipse the Sun of Our Lord will fall from heaven. Then will the

Sign of the Sun of Man flare up in the heavens, and they shall see "the Son of man sitting on the right hand of the power of God, and coming in the clouds of heaven" (Mt. 26:64).

The Judgment Day will be the day of great revelations, not only in the sense that there will be no secrets anymore between persons, but also because it will reveal the secret of Jesus the King to all the world. It will be a sort of new Epiphany, a Feast of the Appearing of the Lord, but more grandiose, more general than the Feast of the Three Kings. It will be a sort of Coronation before all the nations of the earth and all the hosts of heaven.

The notion of the absolute, exclusive, unlimited Kingship of Jesus over the entire human race and the entire universe is one of the most noble, but unfortunately also one of the most forgotten truths of our faith.

We have called the world a book. In this book, Jesus is not only the most interesting and most beautiful chapter, but also the central, dominating idea of the book in its entirety. We must search out this Holy Name on each page and regard everything in its light. When God wanted to call creation into being, He had only one great thought, an immense plan, a dominant idea, one Word: the Word Christ Jesus. Everything that exists has value and meaning in God, only insofar as it is member and organ of the holy Humanity of Jesus, an ornament of the robe of His glory, an image of His perfection, or a footstool for His feet.

St. Paul described the central thought of creation in firm strokes at the beginning of his Epistle to the Colossians: He "is the image of the invisible God, the firstborn of every creature: For in him were all things created in heaven and on earth, visible and invisible, whether thrones, or dominations, or principalities, or powers: all things were created by him and in him. And he is before all, and by him all things consist" (Col. 1:14-17).

Similar expressions are used in the Epistle to the Hebrews: "God...hath spoken to us by his Son, whom he hath appointed heir of all things, by whom also he made the world...For in that he hath subjected all things to him, he left nothing not subject to him" (Heb. 1:1-2; 2:8).

This language leaves us in no doubt. The Kingship of Jesus is not just one chapter, but rather the whole theme of the history of creation and the world. Jesus is all in all.

This idea is even more sharply delineated in St. Paul's teaching on the Church. The Church is the Body of Christ, Christ is the Head of the Church. Head and Body together form an inseparable, mystical, mysterious Unity. The name of this inseparable, mystical Unity is (because the name is taken from the Head) Christ. Christ and His Church, Head and Body bound to one another, says St. Augustine, are only one being, a single Christ. We have not only become Christians. "We are Christ."

"Church" is just another name for Christ united with the members. The Church has its being only in and with and through Him. Christ is all in all, Way, Truth and Life in the Church. The same is true of Church history.

Jesus will be all in all in the fullest sense on Judgment Day. From that day on there will be no more lords and no more kings, there will not even be any more popes. Only one will be Lord, one will be King, one will be the High Priest, "when he shall have brought to nought all principality, and power, and virtue" (I Cor. 15:24). Even the temple will be superfluous in the City of God. "For the Lord God Almighty is the temple thereof, and the Lamb. And the city hath no need of the sun, nor of the moon, to shine in it. For...the Lamb is the lamp thereof" (Apoc. 21: 22-23). So it is written. Everything belongs to Christ. Jesus is all in all. The theme of creation will have reached its completion. Cosmology will become Christology, the study of the world will become the teaching of Christ.

Creation is a book about Jesus the King. "And I saw in the right hand of him that sat on the throne, a book written within and without, sealed with seven seals. And I saw a strong angel, proclaiming with a loud voice: Who is worthy to open the book, and to loose the seals thereof? And no man was able, neither in heaven, nor on earth, nor under the earth, to open the book, nor to look on it. And I wept much, because no man was found worthy to open the book, nor to see it. And one of the ancients said to me: Weep not; behold the lion of Juda, the root of David, hath prevailed to open the book, and to loose the seven seals thereof.

"And the Lamb...came and took the book out of the right hand of him that sat on the throne. And when he had opened the book....they sung a new canticle, saying: Thou art worthy, O Lord, to take the book, and to open the seals thereof; because thou wast slain, and hast redeemed us to God, in thy blood, out of every tribe, and tongue, and people, and nation...And every creature, which is in heaven, and on the earth, and under the earth, and such as are in the sea, and all that are in them: I heard all saying: To the Lamb, benediction, and honor, and glory, and power, for ever and ever" (Apoc. 5:1-5, 7, 9, 13).

Either science will humbly return to Jesus, or the book of creation and of history will remain for science an insoluble riddle. For they tell of Christ. May the song of creation become also the song of mankind: Jesus my King! My Jesus, my All!

Come, let us go there and make Him King, Him alone, King of minds and hearts, the King of the nations as well! Do you hear the bells ringing for the immortal King of the centuries? The world is gradually growing tired of being liberal, far from God and shy of Christ. It is seeking the Sign of the Son of Man. It is seeking the King.

THE KING'S MANIFESTO

It is for me as though Christmas had come again, a great hour of birth, the beginning of a new, strong and more beautiful time. I simply cannot get the Holy Father's encyclical about the Kingship of Christ out of my head. My opinion is that it is a joyous message that belongs to the extraordinary graces of this century. The great Monarch Whom so many have longingly awaited is there. Christ the King! The Christmas manifesto of the eleventh Pius is the proclamation of the world monarchy of the Incarnate God over the peoples!

"And I heard as it were the voice of a great multitude, and as the voice of many waters, and as the voice of great thunders, saying: Alleluia: for the Lord our God the Almighty hath reigned. Let us be glad and rejoice, and give glory to Him...And I saw heaven opened, and behold, a white horse; and He that sat upon him was called faithful and true. His eyes were as a flame of fire, and on His head were many diadems....And out of His mouth proceedeth a sharp, double edged sword, that with it He may strike the nations. And He shall rule them: KING OF KINGS AND LORD OF LORDS" (Apoc. 19:6, 11-12, 15-16).

Long enough has been the word from all the podiums and backstreets: God is dead. Year of death: 1789. The French National Assembly was His Sanhedrin. Since then His official role in the Sanhedrin of the peoples is played out. The Middle Ages are long gone. The world has become liberal. Christ still ekes out an existence in the quiet chamber of private piety or as sacristy deity in a purely religious Catholicism; but as Sovereign of the Nations, as Lawgiver and Judge of the Peoples He has been forced to abdicate. The constitutions no longer know or acknowledge Him. At best He is a private person like any other before the law, but no longer the universal and absolute Monarch. By the state's claim to power and the will of the people, religion and politics are separated and divorced.

The King is dead, says liberal politics. Officially he must not interfere in the temporal affairs of the nations. At least the economy does not use such radical language, although its effects are already disastrous. The economy says: The King does not meddle in our affairs; the King is asleep! The King doesn't see what we're doing. The King is deaf, dumb and lame. Christ does not bother about technology and business in everyday life. Commerce is a neutral zone, beyond good and evil.

Sunday may well belong to God, but weekdays belong to the repairman, the businessman, the farmer, the worker. What does Jesus have to do with the shops and factories, the offices and the department stores? What has He to do with price-fixing and wage questions, with rent contracts and balance-sheets? God is too great to condescend to such little matters. Kings have better things to do. So say Capitalism and Socialism.

The King is not at home. The King is in heaven, sneers so-called education. On earth the professor reigns in His stead, and the school is his kingdom. Faith and science have nothing to do with each other. The classroom must be free territory, untouched by any religious influence and ecclesiastical domination. Each has his place: God in His heaven, the scholar and free researcher in the school! Or however else these people talk.

Like political pride and economic megalomania, academic arrogance doesn't want to hear about the sovereign and general kingship of Christ. Whether one says: the King is dead, or the King is asleep, or the King is absent, the whole modern world together has sworn: We will not have Him rule over us! The same tune as on Good Friday. Social deicide!

And now there comes Pope Pius XI with his encyclical and it sounds like the voice of many waters and the voice of mighty thunderings: Alleluia! The King is not dead, the King lives! The King is not asleep, the King is awake! The King is not absent, the King is still there! Jesus lives, reigns and rules. We proclaim the unlimited, highest, all-embracing Kingship of Jesus not only over all persons, but also over all societies, states, peoples and governments. We proclaim the universal Monarchy of the Crucified over the entire modern world. We oppose 1789 with 1925! God's Bill of Rights against the revolutionary Bill of Human Rights!

The universal kingship of Jesus over human society is no new dogma. It is simply the solemn manifesto of an ancient biblical teaching which is too oft forgotten, but which belongs to that list of undeniable truths without which the human race cannot survive, if it does not want to commit suicide. The second Psalm already seems to have been made to order for the period after 1789. It paints a classic picture of the liberal century: furiously raging nations, peoples in revolt, conspiracies of princes against Christianity, the papacy and canon law make up the content of its history. "Let us break their bonds assunder, and let us cast away their yoke from us" (Ps. 2:3).

In reading the second Psalm one is transported into that summer night when the modern liberties were proclaimed...in vain! "He that dwelleth in heaven shall laugh at them." The ancient God lives yet. The Psalm continues. God holds fast to the universal Kingdom of Jesus even in the face of modern revolution and liberal democracy. The nations are to be the Messiah's inheritance, the "uttermost parts of the earth" for His possession. He shall rule them "with a rod of iron and shall break them in pieces like a potter's vessel." Thus speaks the Psalm.

In the New Testament as well, the theme of the universal messianic kingship is stressed repeatedly. "Art thou a king?" asks Pilate. The answer could not be more explicit: "Thou sayest that I am a king." *Rex sum ego!*—I am a King. And in another solemn moment he repeats: "All power is given to Me in heaven and in earth" (Mt. 28:18). "For he must reign, until he hath put all his enemies under his feet," proclaims St. Paul (I Cor. 15:25). "All things are put under Him" (I Cor. 15:27).

Therefore is Christ the King, King in the complete sense of the word, without any limitations, not even in the sphere of secular power. We have no right to relate the clear texts of both the Old and the New Testament only to the spiritual kingship of Christ. The whole Christ, God and Man, is King, fully and completely, over all things visible and invisible in heaven and on earth. We repeat: Everything is subject to Him! Even politics! Even the economy! Even technology! Even commerce! Even science! Even the arts! The sovereignty of Christ knows no exceptions and no limits!

Christ is the King! He is King over all people: King of the kings! Emperor of the emperors! President of the presidents! Governor of the governments! Lord of the lords! Lawgiver of the lawgivers! Judge of the judges! Christ is King! He is King in word and in truth, not just a decorative figure like the constitutional monarchs. He is not just honorary chairman of the United Nations. He is King not only according to right, but according to might. He really rules. He also uses His enemies, whether they are willing or not, in order to carry out, at least indirectly, His plans, and throws them away, should they resist, like a broken vessel.

Long live Christ the King! Whether we are otherwise republicans or whatnot, in this regard we must all be monarchists, because we are Catholics who have already sworn allegiance to the immortal King of the centuries. The King's banner shall wave on all public squares, over all the schools, all the factories, all the city halls, from all the mountains! If in the future anyone asks us what policy we favor, we shall answer, "We know only one: Long live the King!"

We know that it will not be easy. It is the way of sacrifice. It leads over the Mount of Olives to Calvary, the way to victory. But whoever is not ready to suffer and bleed for a cause is unworthy to live for it. Come! Let us go! *Moriamur pro Christo Rege!*—Let us die for Christ the King!

THE KING'S OPPONENTS

In Rome there is a spiritual Institute of Health. It has the duty of discovering the germs that cause illness in the world of ideas and works. On December 11, 1925, the chairman of this institute, who is responsible for the spiritual health of the whole world, declared in a letter to the shepherds and the peoples: The plague has broken out! It has already attained the proportions of a world epidemic. The name of the plague is laicism.

One might assume that since that December 11, the whole of humanity would have been in an uproar, and that in all the journals of the educated, in all meetings of the people and in all families the epidemic signaled by the Holy Father would be discussed. Everyone who knows the present situation knows that to this day this has not been the case. In general neither the doctors nor the patients have been particularly worried. One can see how far the evil has already progressed from the fact that the sick body's resistance is so weak. Nevertheless, the plague is here! Laicism exists and has become the general illness of our time.

What does "laicism" mean? The Church is, as Pope Pius X teaches in his encyclical *Vehementer* of February 11, 1906, "a society of persons in which a few rule over the rest and possess the full and complete power to lead, to teach and to judge. Accordingly, with regard to power and essence this society is one of inequality, indeed so much so that it contains two states of life, those of the shepherds and the flock, those who belong to the various ranks of the hierarchy and those who belong to the mass of the faithful."

We speak of the shepherds in their various ranks in the hierarchy as the "clergy," which comes from the Greek word *klerisei*, and the flock as the "laity," which derives from another Greek word, *laos*, meaning folk. The layman is thus one from the people, a non-shepherd. So what does laicism do? Even where it does not always radically reject the clerical state, laicism wants this state to disappear more and more from public life. Away with the influence of Church and clergy in public life! Separation of Church and state!

Away with the spirit of Church and clergy, especially from the school! Non-denominational education! Therefore: declericalization! Away from all that is clerical! That is the program of laicism. Laicism is indeed a plague, that is, a deadly disease. The popes have the right of coinage in the kingdom of ideas. They give each thought its correct name and demand, naturally, that every word retain its original meaning or receive it again! No counterfeiting! Therefore, when the Holy Father says that laicism is a plague, then we have no right to view it as only a slight indisposition of modern society. A physician who would treat a serious illness as a harmless weakness would be declared an enemy of the people and a grave-digger. If the pope says "plague," then we must say "plague."

We must not be deceived by the secretive character of the evil. Laicism does not generally operate with the instruments of martyrdom, with fire and sword like the persecutors of the Christians, for example Nero and Diocletian. It has other, much more dangerous methods than the old ones. It takes our oxygen away. It robs us of air. It prevents us from living as Catholics outside of our private rooms and the sacristy. Its method is that of a lung disease: asphyxiation. Laicism is a deadly disease!

Laicism is a plague! It is thus a contagious disease! The danger of contagion is all the greater, because, according to the Holy Father's diagnosis, the bacillus has been "in the blood vessels of the states for a long time," *i.e.,* in the blood of modern society. Laicism belongs, so to speak, to the essence of the modern state. Laicism is its soul, its life principle, its father and its origin. The articles of the constitutions and the paragraphs of the laws may change. But since 1789 one single idea belongs inseparably to their foundations, even if it is not always stated so radically: the state as such, the society as such, the government as such can not and may not be Catholic.

Ask of the modern state what you will; one thing it will never give up, because this thing is its soul, its blood: the idea of independence from Church and clergy, *i.e.,* laicism. That is why the bacillus of laicism spreads almost automatically, like a new original sin, to each new generation, and if a politician is not already infected with it, he is regarded almost as an abnormal and useless person. That is the second reason why laicism must be called a plague.

Laicism is a plague, and therefore it is, as we can see from what has already been said, an epidemic, a world disease. The Holy Father speaks of an infection of human society; he calls laicism in general the plague of our time and thus points to its general spread. Laicism does not stop at any border crossing. It is just as much a German as a French, a Swiss or an Italian disease. Whoever says, "We don't have any laicism," either does not know what he is talking about, or he lies and the truth is not in him.

Therefore the plague of laicism is not just to be found among "the others," but also among us. We are also sick, and the pope has given us the best diagnosis. Laicism has spread as a genuine epidemic to all areas of public life. The pest reigns—as the pope emphasizes particularly—in the city halls, parliaments and congresses. The plague reigns in the courts. The plague has infected the schools. It has art and literature in its grip. The plague reigns—one can hardly believe it—even in works for the common good. To sum up: It has spread so widely that it is easier to say where it does not exist than where it does. It is truly a world-wide epidemic!

Laicism is a plague, and therefore an enemy of the Church and the people! There are enemies whom we must love; this is part of the second great commandment. But there are also enemies whom one must hate. Christ demands this. This hatred is only the reverse side of love. Who cannot really hate, can also not really love. God is love and holiness. That is why He hates with an eternal hatred all that is bad, false, in opposition to God, satanic or revolutionary in His creation. Whoever loves God must hate that which God hates. Whoever loves his fellow men must fight whatever damages mankind: lies and sin in every form and degree.

Gambetta[1] coined the phrase: *"Le clericalisme, voila l'enemi!"*— "Clericalism, there is the enemy!" Since the encyclical of Pope Pius XI we say: "Laicism, there is the enemy, the anti-God, the Antichrist, the anti-Church, the Satan of the century!" Whoever loves this plague hates God, Christ, the Church and the soul. Whoever fails to fight this plague, be it out of laziness, cowardice or lack of interest, becomes a partaker in the guilt for the damage it causes.

---

[1] Leon Gambetta (1838-1882), French liberal statesman.

Therefore we can have but one motto: determined resistance and decisive battle against the plague of the century.

The doctor who gave us the diagnosis of the illness also gave us the prescription. The Holy Father Pius XI declared: "In declaring that Christ shall be honored as King by the entire Catholic world, we wish to meet the need of our times and supply an effective medicine for that plague which has infected human society today." The highest, universal, unlimited Kingship of Christ over state and society is the opposite of modern laicism.

Here, army opposes army, banner against banner, slogan against slogan. We have to choose. We must serve the one side or the other. This is the object of the mighty spiritual battle before which we apparently have arrived. The future belongs either to laicism or to the kingdom of Christ. As far as we are concerned, we believe that the plague, after it has laid waste to the whole earth, will gradually come to an end. Whatever the morrow may bring, the day after tomorrow belongs to Christ the King.

THE KING IN THE DOCK

If God is almighty, why has He not intervened and annulled by decree of His all-highest government every declaration of war? If God is merciful, why does He put up with millions of "innocents" having to shed their blood?

If God is endlessly wise, why does He look on while barbarity and bestiality triumph over a highly developed culture? If God is just, why does He allow all rights of the person, the family and of property be trampled under foot? World wars and world revolutions are not just bankrupt politics; they are also the bankruptcy of religion. If Jesus is King, why doesn't He reign?

That is the charge being brought against Christ today. Mankind in its madness hauls Jesus into court and accuses Him of being the great guilty One for the world wars and for revolution. "Day and night arise from the earth, from its great cities and its lonely dwellings, millionfold complaints, bitter accusations, muffled grumblings, curses and blasphemy against heaven." That is one of the most threatening phenomena in the intellectual life of the present time. Man has fallen into error about the Kingship of Jesus. The foundations of religion have come to tremble in the eyes of the great mass of mankind! It is a childish undertaking for a man to try and make himself God's advocate. Jesus does not need a lawyer. He will plead His case Himself. Yet love for Jesus and the Church, along with love for poor mankind, drives us today to stand up as speaker for the Much-Maligned and His Church against the grumbling masses.

Is the King a failure? First I shall deal with the arguments of the atheists and materialists, the modern unbelievers. They have "explored" the entire vault of heaven and the bowels of the earth, they have burrowed in all the archives of the world and studied the miniscule atom, in order to find proof against the existence of God. They tell us that the question is scientifically settled: There is no God! Everything is eternal matter and eternal force!

No greater paradox is imaginable. You don't curse someone who does not exist. That would be ridiculous. A sensible atheist, if there can be such a thing as an atheist with good sense, cannot be a blasphemer. He does not believe in God. Therefore he does not talk about Him and about Jesus. Therefore we have a right to demand *a priori* that all those who deny God hold their tongues on the question of whether Jesus has failed.

The second class in the society of the critics of God and Jesus consists of the so-called liberals. They may perhaps still believe in a Supreme Being, but they claim that this Being, once He created the world, went into retirement! God has abdicated! Liberalism forbids Him any interference in the course of political events. The politicians and diplomats are supposedly free of responsibility, independent and sovereign! Jesus has nothing more to say in the temporal affairs of the nations! That is a liberal dogma, and when a Catholic priest once preached from the pulpit against this dogma, liberalism protested his interference in the affairs of the state.

What happened? World War I began in 1914. In the whole world there was no Catholic government. All of them without exception had become more or less liberal. It seemed as though Jesus Himself had become "liberal" in order to punish the nations: He did not "interfere in the political affairs of the nations." He apparently did what all the popular assemblies and the newspapers had been demanding of Him for more than a hundred years. And now look at the paradox! The nations which had been liberal for a century and which had given themselves liberal constitutions and elected liberal representatives now accused God of committing a crime, because He did not want to interfere in politics! If one is liberal, then one has no right to accuse God of non-intervention. If the liberals want to be consistent, then they have to keep silence on our question.

A word to the sentimental souls: The World Wars and the revolutions with all their injustices that cry to heaven and all their cruelties are supposed to be proof that there is no God, and that Jesus is a failure. Answer: The world has not only become unbelieving and liberal; it is godless. Of course, there have always been godless individuals. But it has been reserved to modern times to raise godlessness to public power. And what is worse, godlessness has turned into actual glowing hatred of God. It became a fury. Mankind fell upon God in order to strangle Him, kill Him and eradicate Him.

Whoever casts a glance into the secrets of modern Freemasonry knows that we are not exaggerating. Freemasonry is the secret government behind most of the earth's governments. What we are experiencing since the French Revolution is the radical, implacable, irreconcilable war against God, the revolution of earth against heaven.

If this is the case, what did God have to do? All graces had been thrown to the wind, all warnings were ridiculed. The world had become unteachable and incapable of conversion. God's mercy and patience were only taken as an excuse for more impertinence and new ridicule. And it must be emphasized that we stood it! We watched the outbreaks of hatred against God and had no laws and no courts with which to defend the rights of God and His Christ. We made ourselves accomplices.

God had to speak, in order to preserve His rights on His earth. He had to resort to last means. He had to. We may not allow any difficulties whatsoever to shake our faith in God. But if there were anything which could have awakened doubts in us as to the existence of God, then it would have been if there had been no answer to the horrendous modern hatred of God and war against God.

One author has written: "As for me, I admit that I never felt the nearness, the presence of God, so immediately as during the war years. Whoever does not now believe in God, he will perhaps believe in Him tomorrow. Whoever does not believe tomorrow will believe the day after tomorrow. God can speak so loudly that all ears ring from His *Ephphetha.*"

Christ gives a course in apologetics on the theme of His Kingship, and He will not terminate it until He has achieved His goal, which is that all the world comprehend that God exists, and that He reigns with endless wisdom, love and righteousness.

The ancient God lives still, by the way. The greatest criminal courts cannot erase the picture that Holy Scripture paints of Him. He came into the world in order to redeem us. He lay in the manger as a poor Child. He was friend of the lowly, the poor, the sick and the sinners. He let Himself be scourged, crowned with thorns and crucified out of immeasurable love. He gave us the most holy Sacrament, in order to dwell with us forever. He gave us the power to become children of God. He promises us the whole of heaven with its endless joys in exchange for a few years of suffering and work.

He gives us innumerable physical goods, which He pours out over the just and the unjust, although He owes us not a penny, not a crumb, not a ray of sunshine. The ancient God lives still. The eternal light still burns before our tabernacles. Whoever claims that such a God is loveless, unjust and cruel, whoever speaks of Him as though He were the enemy of the human race, whoever grumbles against God, is a monster of ingratitude.

The grumbling of the nations is also directed against Jesus' Church. She, the Church with the pope, is the second accused in the dock, who is supposed to be a failure. The charge is of immense seriousness. The more victims fall in this time of catastrophes, the more do the truly guilty shove off the responsibility onto the Catholic Church. In the coming cultural battle, all the rogues and deceivers of this earth will drag the Church as cause of all unhappiness up the hill of Calvary, in order to stone and crucify her. They claim that the Church has failed!

No one could speak more thoughtlessly and unjustly. After all, who reigns over the entire internal and foreign policy of the nations? Who holds the modern school in his grip and educates the men who tomorrow will lead the destinies of Europe? Who controls economic life, industry, trade, the banks and the stock market?

Who has all the news agencies of the world and the entire mass media—this queen of public opinion—under his thumb? Liberalism, that is laicism, atheism, capitalism, Freemasonry, materialism, nationalism, militarism.

I emphasize once again: there may well exist Catholics, even Catholic areas, but as far as I know there is at this time in the whole of Europe not a single Catholically governed state, not a single really Catholic government.

The Church enjoys a certain respect. But in reality she is bound hand and foot. Nearly everywhere her bishops are treated as lackeys by the state. Her visible head, the pope, was for years a prisoner in the Vatican. You hypocrites! You "storm with rough infantry, light cavalry and heavy artillery over our fields, just when the fruit is ripening," and then you accuse us of not having full harvests! You shut our mouths with your laws and decrees, and then you criticize us because we do not speak out. You rob us of our Church property, our monasteries and convents, and then you accuse us of not being socially involved.

You nail us to the cross, and then you mock us because we do not climb down. You hypocrites, give our pope, our bishops, our priests, our laity unlimited freedom to speak, to act, to live as we wish, and then come and see if we fail! And in the meantime beat your own sinful breasts and admit that you and all your fundamentals have failed to the extent of complete bankruptcy.

Grumbling against Christ is madness! It is one of the greatest and most sinister sins. It is the sin that regards God as an enemy. When one errs about God, then the foundation of religion collapses.

Oh, I understand: there are hours in the life of a person when the deep, dark night of despair wraps the soul, and the perplexed spirit is bowed down to earth by a monstrous heaviness. Still, in such hours on the Mount of Olives faith must not falter. Even when we cannot see the way forward, we must let ourselves be led by the hand of Christ, like children, thinking: Jesus knows the way. He still reigns today.

That suffices. And when my understanding fails, I shall still bow it before the Incomprehensible. I shall believe and hope. With Job, the great sufferer, I shall say: "I shall lay mine hand upon my mouth" (Job 39:34). I shall keep silence. Night and clouds will pass away. God does not die. God does not fail. Jesus does not fail. The true Church does not fail. The eternal light of our tabernacles is not yet extinguished. It will become the dawning light of a new day.

NO ROOM FOR THE KING

Nobody in Bethlehem had basically anything against the new citizen Christ. But the political, social and economic conditions led to there being no room for the Messiah.

Where would Christ be born today? Doesn't the question of room for the Christchild today cause us so much pondering that we would be heartily glad to have the neutral ground of the stable?

Haven't we politicians, sociologists, economists, intellectuals and artists committed the crime of Bethlehem for at least the last hundred years? Does not the liberal sin consist in limiting, for lack of room, the universally present Christianity of past times to certain holy reservations?

Christ's Truth is all-present, all-applicable, permanent, like the source of daylight, the sun. It is everywhere or nowhere. It is exclusively and completely sun, or it is nonexistent. It is for everyone or no one. One lives through it and dies without it. Christ the King needs too much room, in other words, all of it. That is His "misfortune"! His Truth wants not only to live, but to reign absolutely and alone. Here is the reason why Christ would be born today, as then, in a stable.

Certainly He would not be born in City Hall. The government has to tread very softly on the parquetry of non-denomenationalism. It may not place itself one-sidedly in the service of a particular "party," especially one which is extreme besides! If only Christ had been just plain "Christian!" But he was Roman Catholic: He believed in miracles, in the Holy Trinity, in the primacy of the pope, and even defined in Matthew (16:18) the Ultramontanist dogma of infallibility! For constitutional reasons, therefore, the application of the heavenly Father for making room for Bethlehem in City Hall must be turned down. Of course no one denies the cultural value of Christianity. However, the project of the so-called Redemption absolutely must be carried out on the basis of the existing state law. "Because there is no room there for a king."

In view of the fact that Christ is the incarnate, eternal Wisdom, perhaps Heaven would try to win over the college as the birthplace of Christ. The Senate would then consider in a lengthy meeting the problem of whether Christ may be born on the college campus. Surely it would be pointed out that one is in step with "God" in striving for the "higher things." On the other hand, the purely scientific character of the university ought not to be put in question by allowing religion to be mixed into it. Therefore the application must be rejected, "because there is no room."

An application to the academy of arts would have no better chance. Today literature, painting, music, *etc.*, have merely artistic goals. Influence on the arts through non-artistic tendencies must not be permitted. It is true that religion has provided much subject-material for the arts; nevertheless, art must not close itself to the endless realm of the beautiful by selling itself to one particular direction. Art is no more Catholic than color, canvas or paper! Christ wants too much room! He wants the catholic space, *i.e.,* everything!

St. Joseph, give it a try, shyly and quietly. Do you see those big storehouses, factories, banks? There must be room over there! "Wrong! Those are the castles of pure economy! There they ask us: What does Christ have to do with coal, iron and silk?" St. Joseph protests with a quote from the first question in the Catholic Catechism, the fundamental question of the generous Catholic "world view." The pure economists propose for tactical reasons that besides Christ other "Christian" religious founders be given room in economic life. Since St. Joseph is not willing to accept this compromise, Christ the King must out of tactical considerations remain outside. No room!

Besides the purely political, purely economic and purely artistic sectors, there are also the fields of pure entertainment and pure sociology, where Christ naturally also has not much say. Whether on principle or for tactical reasons, one sector after another has been withdrawn from the sphere of influence of Catholic truth. There is no more room for the King.

We find the deicide on Golgotha more honest and masculine than this robbery of air, light and room to the point of asphyxiation. Even if a person means well in his use or his permitting of these tactics, it changes nothing in the final ruin of our cause. Of what help to us is it, when one lets us live in principle but kills us tactically? Of what use is a kingdom without land? Make room for the omnipresent God! How much room? All of it!

THE KING WITHOUT A CROWN

Concerning our society today, we must affirm that Jesus does not reign any longer. They have taken away His crown and scepter. Everyday life has almost completely excluded the supernatural. The world is dechristianized, naturalized, ecologized and far from Jesus—not only the part of the world whose population is 99% heathen, but also the regions whose population is 99% Christian. As soon as one leaves the church and perhaps also the family living-room, one generally does not notice that one lives among Christians.

Fifty years ago Cardinal Mermillod could already exclaim: "The notion of the supernatural—who has it anymore? It is almost nonexistent!" Since then, the possibility of finding Jesus anywhere in society, except in the tabernacles and in the hearts of a few pious souls, has become even more remote.

As usual, it all began in the world of ideas. Modern man's world of ideas is empty of God. The concepts of God, of Jesus, of eternity become rarer and rarer, until finally they have almost disappeared. Faith is falling asleep. Its light has gone out. Its voice is silent. It is not dead, but it has ceased to be the eye and the voice of the soul. The world of thought for most Christians during their daily work hardly differs from that of the better heathens in the times before Christ: some common sense, some naturally good ideas, some sincerity. But in general it is a world without Jesus. Therefore it is a cold, empty world.

No better than the world of ideas is the world of words. A person says what he thinks. What fills the heart overflows through the mouth, the mouth and the pen. A world which for whole hours, days and weeks never thinks of Jesus, His person, His teachings and

His laws, will of course not talk about Him. In fact, there is probably no name which is more carefully avoided in conversation among Christians as the Name of Jesus.

Fr. Weiss was right: We talk about everything, except for the one Name in Whom everything is included. We are proud of every little nothing, but if He, before Whom every knee should bow, is even mentioned, it is almost as though we were ashamed of Him. A person meets another person, a Christian another Christian, and what do they talk about? The weather, politics, money, business, sports, fashion, "her" or "him." If anyone would have the courage to bring up—naturally, out of the urging of his heart—the Name of Jesus, the others would be aghast. You don't talk about Him!

A certain man who knows his times well has raised the question: How many times a year in all the parliaments of so-called Christian Europe, in which supposedly the peoples with their views and opinions are represented, is the Name of Jesus mentioned? How often does one talk about Jesus? It would not surprise us if even in good Catholic circles one answered with a pitying smile and the exclamation: What does Jesus have to do with parliaments, and what have parliaments to do with Jesus?!

"Poor Jesus!" St. Alphonsus would say. To this we've come with our so-called Christianity! Everyday speech has been de-christianized more and more, especially that of the politicians and the businessmen. It is a language without Jesus, a language that every decent heathen would also use. It is outside the supernatural. It is more than modern: it is modernistic.

As with the realms of thought and words, so it is with the world of deeds. You can praise modern technology as much as you will. Jesus is generally not with it. It has no Christian soul. It does not believe in Him, Who made everything. It doesn't pray. It does not sing and rejoice before the great God, but instead plays at being properly neutral, nondenominational, if it does not openly make fun of Him.

In earlier times work was done before the cross and the picture of the Madonna. It was oriented towards Heaven. It was worship, penance, a matter of conscience, the imitation of Christ, the practice of obedience, of patience, of love of one's neighbor. It was assumed into the world of the supernatural. Nowadays not only the crucifix is missing in the workshops, the official bureaus and the business offices; the spirit is missing as well. Jesus doesn't reign anymore. The exceptions only prove the rule.

Jesus must reign again, not only in the churches, but also in the workshop, in our families, in our festivities, in all the streets and public squares, in our city halls and our schools. The life of Christians, which has become completely naturalistic and purely secular, must become supernatural again. The miracle of Cana must be repeated in our present society. Figuratively speaking, we have no more wine. We only drink the tasteless, lukewarm water of the cisterns of the spirit of the world and the times.

Christ must transform the water of naturalism into the wine of the supernatural. Here the marriage of Cana is a sign of what ought to happen now. The miracle of Cana is a miracle of transformation. The world ought not only to be improved, but also transformed; not simply renewed, but completely changed. Not just "reformation" or "renewal" should be the motto, but rather "transformation." All that is purely worldly, simply natural and earthly must become by God's grace spiritual, supernatural, heavenly.

When a priest comes to the Offertory, he prays while blessing the water: "O God, Who hast wonderfully created the dignity of human nature and yet more wonderfully renewed it, grant us that through the mystery of this water and wine we may partake of the Divinity of Him Who condescended to partake of our humanity, Jesus Christ, Thy Son, our Lord, Who liveth and reigneth with Thee in the unity of the Holy Spirit...." As often as we assist at Holy Mass, this miracle of transformation takes place at the altar, the transformation of the natural into the supernatural, the mortal into the immortal, bread and wine into the Body and Blood of Christ.

During the Mass we should not and must not be simply passive witnesses of this transformation. We should live it. The human being in us should "become Christ." Every person who goes home after the *Ite missa est* should be another person than the one who tapped his breast during the *Confiteor*. He should be a person with another soul, another heart, other eyes, another tongue, other hands: a supernatural person inside and outside.

I particularly stress: a person with other eyes. We must view everything completely differently. We must see with the eyes of faith, with the eyes of Heaven, with the eyes of eternity, with the eyes of Jesus. Everything as Jesus says, everything as Jesus wills it, everything as Jesus makes it! That is Christianity! The water should become wine. Then the King will regain His scepter and His crown.

Everything in the wide world happens today only naturally. That is why nothing goes right anymore. Everything must be different. Jesus must again reign over us, everywhere, always. That is why our prayer in our great need can be no other than the prayer at the end of the Apocalypse: Come, Lord Jesus! Let the answer of Our Lord to His beloved disciple be fulfilled in us also: Surely I come quickly!

THE KING IN THE CRIB

"That's a mystery! I just don't understand it!" Three gentlemen are standing (they can't kneel) before Christ's crib, the Three Kings of modern culture, the modern professor, the modern businessman, the modern statesman. As long as you talk about the crib in the context of cultural history, they are somewhat interested. The story is so poetic! The little baby surrounded by shepherds and lambs—isn't that just lovely!

However, if you go further and point out that this Child is the Son of the Living God, Himself God and King of the human race, then the scene is suddenly regarded in a different light. The representatives of the modern worldview start looking at the Christchild's inventory: a rented stable, a manger, swaddling clothes. Then they shake their heads in unison: "We just can't understand it!"

The sole inventory of a King being a stable, a crib, a diaper—not only do we not understand it, not only is it a mystery, but a protest against our entire modern culture! If this Child is right, then all of modern culture is confusion, insanity, in its consequences an incalculable heresy. What is modern culture? Megalomania, worship of the golden calf, pride of power. What is the crib? Humility, poverty, weakness. These are opposites between which we must choose.

The little King in the crib is a protest against megalomania. With this mania began the misery in paradise. The banner of science was raised before the eyes of our first ancestors. Your eyes will be opened! You'll be like gods! At the sound of the trumpet of the Enlightenment, the whole structure of Adam's virtues collapsed. As soon as the talk turned to "education," faith and obedience fell apart. Since then pride of education is in our blood. All revolutions against God and the Church, all apostasy from the faith and all sectarianism have come about under this banner. The most monstrous nonsense is worshipped by the public, as long as you call it scientific.

Even among us there are many who promise themselves a paradise on earth through science. They think that it suffices to enlighten people in order to improve them. Nothing is further from the truth. The angel who knew the most fell deepest. "Lucifer" (light bearer) has become the devil.

The question has been asked as to which belief has produced the most despicable elements, the greatest monstrosities, the most bloodthirsty revolutions. I should not be surprised if one could prove on the basis of history that the majority of them were fallen-away Catholics who as children had to learn their whole catechism by heart. One falls deepest from the highest mountains.

Which period in history should be characterized as the most barbaric? The one that built the most palatial schools and libraries, the one in which the most was read and in which the schoolyears were the longest: the twentieth century! Which clan is the most immoral? The one which knows the most, the one in which the children learned the most at the youngest age about "the birds and the bees." When has the family been at its lowest ebb? Now, when more parents-and-teachers meetings, more household and motherhood preparation courses are arranged than ever before. When has the citizen had the least love for his home country? Now, after he has been politically enlightened for more than a hundred years under the reign of Liberalism by the wisdom of the statesmen, civics classes and party conventions.

The world wars, which brought the collapse of very many things on this earth, were also the bankruptcy of science. Only after people had learned so much about chemistry, electricity, transport technology on land, sea and in the air, could the great genocide begin. Knowledge, and with it the book, the school, the library are, we dare to say, neither the first nor the most important cause. We do not want to be misunderstood: we would not keep the people in ignorance in order to govern them better.

We stress only the truth: Science is not the first, but the second thing, not the necessary, but the secondary matter. We take the point of view of the Child in the crib: "Amen, I say to you, except you...become as little children, you shall not enter into the kingdom of heaven. Whosoever therefore shall humble himself as this little child, he is the greater in heaven" (Mt. 18:3-4). Humble, childlike faith is more sensible and gives more joy to the peoples than all of science. The professor, *i.e.,* proud and one-sided education, has failed.

The Christchild, the poor Christchild, is a protest against luxury and the service of mammon. If a person is innerly poor, he tries to balance out his inner poverty through external goods like clothes, jewelry, houses, property. Because he has lost the inner paradise, he tries to make the outer world into a paradise. That is the proud program of Liberalism and Socialism. The liberal program says: "Paradise for the upper ten thousand!" The socialist program says: "Paradise for everybody!"

Both liberals and socialists are in error. They search, despite all the lessons of six thousand years of history, at the wrong time and in the wrong place and are therefore condemned to search forever and never to find. They search at the wrong time, because the first Paradise disappeared six thousand years ago and the second Paradise will only begin after Judgment Day. They look in the wrong place, because Paradise, if one can exist at all in the period between the Fall and Judgment Day, is not external, but internal, in the heart. If in our hearts the hell of discontent burns, then all fine clothes, jewels, houses and property are of no use. If in our hearts the heaven of happiness laughs, then all our earthly goods are of no importance.

The poor Christchild is the rejection of Liberalism, Socialism, and the Materialism common to both of them. The poor Christchild says: As far as true wealth and truly lasting happiness are concerned, external goods play only a small or subsidiary role. A swaddling cloth, a crib and a stable are enough. Before God and one's conscience the only true wealth is that which one is, not that which one has. Our God is named Jehovah, Yahweh, which means He

Who Is, not He Who Has. On this principle rests the wisdom of the crib: The Christmas ideal of Christianity is not he who has something, but he who is something.

While among the heathens and in the distorted type of Judaism earthly goods have the highest stock values, at the sound of the angels' Gloria over the fields by Bethlehem they experience their deepest market crash. They are devaluated. St. Paul expressed it in drastic terms: "But the things that were gain to me, the same I have counted as loss for Christ...and count them but as dung, that I may gain Christ" (Phil. 3: 7-8).

Modern culture, which is completely heathen, has once again driven the stocks of earthly goods to record heights. The world war had the assignment of pulling them back down to the true, God-willed value. According to an old prophecy which seems to me perfectly plausible, the result of a world war must be bankruptcy of the states and the peoples. The ideal of the future ought not to be the person who has something, as it is now, but rather the person who is something. That will be the victory of the King in the crib over modern big capital as well as liberal and socialist materialism.

The weak Christchild is a protest against the display of power by human force. The two basic truths of religion are the truth about God and the truth about man. The truth about God and about man is as follows: God is endlessly great, man endlessly small. In the words of the Bible: God "hath measured the waters with the hollow of His hand and weighed the heavens with His palm. He hath poised with three fingers the bulk of the earth and weighed the mountains in scales, and the hills in a balance." Before Him the nations are "as a drop of a bucket...behold, the islands like a little dust." He reigns over the earth, "and the inhabitants thereof are as locusts before him." "All flesh is grass and the glory thereof as the flower of the field. The grass is withered, and the flower is fallen, because the spirit of the Lord hath blown upon it. Indeed the people is grass" (*Cf.* Is. 40:6-7, 12, 15, 22).

"Thus saith the Lord: Cursed be the man that trusteth in man, and maketh flesh his arm, and whose heart departeth from the Lord. He shall be like tamarick in the desert" (Jer. 17:5-6). Pride in one's own strength and displays of power are abominations in the sight of the Lord. Who is stronger, the child or the man? Humanly speaking, the man in his maturity is stronger. Divinely speaking it is the child, that is, the person who places all his trust in God alone. We see this illustrated by King Herod and the Child Jesus. One would almost say that God takes particular pleasure in putting down the mighty.

"The day of the Lord of hosts shall be upon every one that is proud and highminded, and upon every one that is arrogant, and he shall be humbled. And upon all the tall and lofty cedars of Lebanon, and upon all the oaks of Basan. And upon all the high mountains and upon all the elevated hills. And upon every high tower, and every fenced wall" (Is. 2:12-15). That is the teaching of the crib, and because the crib did not suffice, it is the teaching of the world wars. In both, in the crib and in the war, God wanted to prove to man that he is weak, and that he ought honestly to admit his weakness. God hates the proud, puffed up, self-reliant, self-confident display of power, whether political or social.

An old legend tells that when the Christchild came to Egypt, all the heathen idols fell in ruins. This miracle has got to happen again today. Before this Child all the heathen idols, which are much more numerous today than in the heathen nations of old, must fall down! The little Child Jesus must be the Victor over modern pride of knowledge! The poor Child Jesus must be victor over modern materialism! The weak Child Jesus must triumph over modern pride of power! God will pound our present ideals to dust. We shall have to begin again. We shall have to re-learn everything. The school of the new peoples will be the crib. The Teacher will be the tiny, poor, weak Christchild! Let us all go there and make Him King, King of our minds, King of our hearts, King of our families, King of the nations.

THE KING'S RIGHTS

When the sun goes down behind the mountains, the night does not begin immediately. The light remains for a time over the land, and only gradually do the shadows deepen into complete darkness. Nietzsche, the philosopher of the Superman, pointed to this phenomenon in order to explain why many non-believers still carry Christian ideas in themselves and act in a Christian way.

Their Sun has set, but it is not yet midnight, the hour of darkness. It is the time in which day and night flow into one another, the twilight of the soul.

In the life of the peoples we can observe the same phenomenon. In the sixteenth century began for many the sundown of Christianity. But it is not yet midnight. It is only sundown. The Sun of Jesus has disappeared behind the great cloud-mass of Rationalism and Materialism. The so-called modern world no longer believes, but it still lives from the reserves of Christian attitudes and Christian morals from the thousand Catholic years of Europe.

I don't like this twilight period. It is the time of the halfhearted and the cowards. I prefer the night, the complete blackness. I love the day, the clear light. I love the whole, the radically honest belief—and if someone does not believe anymore, then I hold radical, honest atheism to be more masculine. I stand today before the crib, but not because it is the custom. I stand there, because in this manger lies all my theology, my philosophy, my social policy and my teaching.

What does this Child want? His Christmas program, which is at the same time the school curriculum of all centuries, has been half locked away, half counterfeited. That half of the Christmas message which has been locked up in a cupboard, and with it all the art of instruction and education, is the Gloria. Glory be to God! That was the morning prayer of the Christchild, and the first Christmas hymn was a Te Deum!

In the beginning God created heaven and earth: One God, One Lord, the Lord of Lords, Who rules over His creation with immeasurable Majesty. All creatures are the possession of Him Who created them! Man belongs to God! Exclusively and completely! That is why the morning prayer of mankind in Paradise can be nothing other than the Gloria: Glory be to God!

Mankind did not want to sing it anymore. For four thousand years mankind had busied himself with all sorts of things: science, art, handwork, politics, war. But he had forgotten the Gloria, the morning prayer of his first ancestors, the eternal prayer of the stars and the flowers.

Then came the Child Jesus, and the first thing He taught mankind, the first subject of His world education, was the Gloria. One of the great revolutions of world history began with the declaration of the rights of man, just as the first of all revolutions began with Satan's declaration of human rights over and against God. The salvation of mankind, the opposite of revolution, would therefore also begin with Christ's reminder and proclamation of the Rights of God. That is the meaning of the Gloria. God is God! Man is man! God is the Lord! Mankind is His servant! Creation belongs to the Creator! Property belongs to the Owner! Glory be to God!

God's rights are above human rights. Glory be to God on high! That is the deepest sense of religion. That is religion! The modern religious founders overlooked that. They founded religions whose main purpose is the formation of hardworking, patient, sober people. They founded religions which are charitable organizations, in which the love of neighbor is everything. In these matters they did what true religion must do, but they neglected the first and foremost thing. The main emphasis of Christianity lies on the first of the two Tables of the Law. The first table contains the rights of God. God must be God! The sovereignty of God should be proclaimed without reservation, in all times and places, everywhere. That is the most necessary thing which must be said from the pulpits today.

The great sin of science, of the school, the elementary but most especially the secondary schools and the college, the sin of art, the sin of politics and the sin of commercial life, the real sin of the century is this: They do not pray the Gloria anymore. They refuse to acknowledge God, even if they do not specifically deny Him. They are atheistic, godless.

We have learned to know the Christmas message of the Divine Child. And what is ours? Answer: We must see that the Gloria is sung again everywhere in the whole world, in the city halls, in the schools and universities, in the factories. We must ring the Christmas bells, the bells of the King.

The Christians do not see, do not hear and do not speak. We have to wake them up. The Christians are nervous like all modern people, but the Christians can't be aroused to anger for their God. When will that Christmas come when the Gloria again becomes an angry battle cry against all denial of God and all blasphemy against God?

We must ring the bells. They call to work. For our God and our Church the nineteenth century was a century of robbery. From His earth that was made by Him, one kingdom after another was taken. The world has been de-clericalized. The world was stolen from God and God from the world. We must make restitution and reparation! The twentieth century ought to have been the century of restitution in all areas, in which the world was returned to its Owner, even down to the last penny!

The ancient Christmas carol must become truth once again. The song of science must become the Gloria to the Eternal Wisdom; the song of technology must be the Gloria and Te Deum to the God Who made heaven and earth! The battle song of politics must be the Gloria to Him Who sitteth upon the throne, and unto the Lamb!

The sovereignty of God must be won back without reservation.

We argue over the right tactics, but there is only one: the policy of the Gloria. If we with all our cleverness make half the world happy but act against the interests of God in the process, then all our politics of realism and success will bring us nothing. Even if our tactic brings us, like the Christchild, to Calvary, then it is still the right one so long as it seeks God.

Our policy consists in praying the Gloria.

THE KING OF THE CHURCH

All feastdays of the Church year are Catholic feastdays. This is true of the papal feast in a special way, because the pope is the proper mark of Christianity, a king of the kings and lord of the lords, a father of the peoples. With the pope stands or falls Christianity, just as the body stands or falls with the head. If it were possible to destroy the papacy, Catholicism would immediately cease to exist, even if it still numbered five hundred million members. We are therefore either papal or we are nothing. The liberal differentiation between Catholics and "papists" is nonsense. Catholics who are not papists are traitors. Their place is outside the bounds of canon law.

When we call the pope the mark of Catholicism, our spiritual king, we do not forget to add that the pope, regardless of how great his dignity may be, is actually only a vicar. In that we regard the

pope as Vicar of Christ, that is, as His deputy, we declare specifically that the true, living, though invisible King of the Church is
Christ, just as the true and actual bishop of a diocese or the actual
rector of a parish is Christ. The bishops and parish priests are His
representatives.

Here we come to the innermost essence of the Church. Whoever sees nothing more than a society of likeminded people in the
Church, who are led by a clerical hierarchy, knows nothing of what
the Church is, or he knows it only superficially. He knows the
Church only from the outside, not from the inside. The deepest explanation of the Church was given by St. Paul, when he calls Christ
the Head of the Church and the Church the Body of Christ. Christ
is the King of the Church!

As Paul writes in the Epistle to the Ephesians, God "hath subjected all things under his feet and made him the head over all the
Church, which is His Body..." (Eph. 1:22-23). It is impossible to
illustrate the relationship between Christ and Church more inti-
mately than is done with these words. It means the permanent,
all-embracing dependence of the Church on Christ the King.

This dependence is not only historical, in the sense that the
Church exists because she was founded by Christ, but could then
continue to exist by herself, like a work of art which did not exist
before it was made by the artists continues to exist without the artist
after its creation.

The dependence of the Church on Christ is much more an uninterrupted bond, so that the Church would immediately cease to
exist, were Christ to withdraw from her for even one moment. The
Church can survive from the death of a pope to the election of the
next pope for a few days, weeks, perhaps in a time of persecution
for many months, but she cannot survive for a single second without her invisible Head, without Christ the King.

Therefore the activity of the Church with regard to its magisterium, its episcopal hierarchy and its priesthood is completely dependent. Christ is the Head of the Church. From this follows that
the Head thinks, the Head speaks—not the body. Everything depends upon the King. Whatever the Church presents as that which
must be believed, must be His word. The Church has no right to
declare anything else as dogma. The Church in her relationship to

us is our teacher, but only under the condition that she first sit as pupil at the feet of the Lord.

In His words of farewell Christ says: "...The Spirit of Truth...shall not speak of himself, but what things soever he shall hear, he shall speak....He shall receive of mine, and shew it to you" (Jn. 16:13-14). Therefore the authority of the magisterium and the infallibility of the pope rest in the final analysis on the presence of Jesus: "Lo, I am with you always, even unto the end of the world." The pope is only infallible under the condition of his complete dependence upon Jesus, the teacher, and only as vicar, as representative of the infallible Christ the King.

The same applies to the bishops. The bishop is not independent. The pope and, far more, the bishop and the priest can not do whatever they want to. Christ is the Head, Christ commands, Christ reigns. The King makes the decisions. As successor to St. Peter the pope possesses a fullness of power greater than that of the mightiest emperor. But even the pope can only issue orders insofar as he as vicar has first taken orders from Jesus Christ. The Head and only the Head reigns, but the Head of the Church is Christ.

How much greater is the absolute dependence of the priesthood! Priesthood is service to sacrifice and the mediating of grace, the dispensation of supernatural life through the sacraments. Dispensation of supernatural life is an exclusively divine privilege. Only He who can say: "I am...the Life. No man cometh to the Father, but by Me" (Jn. 14:6), can dispense it. Certainly, priests are dispensers of grace, but they are such only as servants, as instruments, channels, and not as actual cause and source. There is no altar without Christ, no baptismal font without Christ, no confessional without Christ. The King is everything.

Life comes from the head, not from the tongue, not from the hand, not from the body. Without Christ the Head, we priests would all say only empty words at the altar, the font or in the confessional. Without Christ neither the simple priest, nor the bishop, nor the pope can have the least priestly effect. Here we see how wrong the Church's detractors are when they claim that we in the Catholic Church shove Christ aside.

We cannot make ourselves lower than when we says that we are nothing of our own strength. And we can raise Christ no higher than when we say: Christ is Head of the Church. We are only instruments. We are only voices and channels of grace. It is the King Who does everything.

Yet we must proclaim another truth. Humility must not go so far that it becomes a lie. Not only is Christ Head and King of the Church; the Church is also the Body of Christ. The Church is Queen. That is a dogma of incalculable consequences! We are not talking about the physical Body of the Lord. Since the Resurrection, the physical Body of Christ is unchangeable in its glorious immortality.

What we call the Church is far more a mystical, mysterious, supernatural organism, whose members are the faithful, whose Head is Christ and whose "soul" is the Holy Spirit. When St. Paul calls the Church the body of Christ, he teaches that Christ and the Church form a single, collective being, the whole Christ. The whole Christ is, as St. Augustine remarks, head and body, the only begotten, incarnate Son of God, the body of the Church (*De unitate ecclesiae*).

Just as there can be no body without a head, so there is no head without a body. Just as there can be no Church without Christ, so there is no Christ without the Church, no King without the Queen. The body is the organism through which the head works. The Church is in its members, the priests, the teachers, the shepherds and the rest of the faithful the organism of Christ. The head can work only through the body. Christ works in humanity only through the Church.

Because Christ is the Way, the Truth and the Life, because without Christ one can do nothing supernaturally good, because no one comes to the Father except through Him, yet Christ works only through His Body, the Church is therefore the only means to salvation. She is the way, the truth and the life, without which one can do nothing supernaturally good. No one comes to the King except through the Queen.

All truth of supernatural order which is in the world, including that to which non-Catholic confessions still hold, came into the world through her. Every grace received by anyone at all, be he Catholic or Protestant, Jew or heathen, he receives through the prayers, the holy sacrifices, the penitential works and the blessings of the Church. If any soul, living outside the Church but in error through no fault of its own, comes into heaven, then it is thanks to Christ in Heaven working through His Mystical Body the Church.

The words, "Outside the Church no salvation," are valid without any exceptions, because there can be no exception to the other words, "No salvation without Christ." No other religion outside of the Church has saved a single soul or mediated a single grace for nineteen hundred years. For even the baptism given in other confessions was only valid insofar as it was dispensed unconsciously in the name of the Church. Spiritually the whole world lives from the Church, because the whole world lives from Christ; Christ and the Church, however, are one and the same thing, the whole Christ, the Head with the Body, the King with the Queen.

I conclude: What is valid for all is valid for us as well. The baptismal certificate alone is not enough. The proof that we have paid our taxes is less than enough. Only practicing Catholicism saves: faith, love, deeds, union with Christ the King and His Church the Queen, union with the pope, the King's visible image and likeness. Christ, Church, St. Peter, all belong together. Whoever tries to separate them, does not know them. What God has bound together, man shall not tear asunder. Therefore, whoever as opponent of modern laicism holds high the banner of Christ the King must also stand in principle and in fact for the monarchy of the Church and Her Head. Long live the King! Long live the Queen! Long live the pope!

THE KING'S BRIDE

The Marriage at Cana: As important as a Christian marriage may be for the renewal of human society, at Cana much more was at stake. The couple at Cana are actually only models and signs. Their marriage gave Jesus the opportunity at the beginning of His public ministry to reveal the great mystery and goal of His Incarnation: the marriage of the King's Son, the union of God with mankind. The Son of Heaven came down to earth so that the sons of earth could rise up to heaven. The work of redemption is nothing less than the marriage of mankind with the Son of God. Thus does

Jesus appear at Cana as the Divine Bridegroom Whose bride, the Church that is coming into being, is led to Him.

Only now can we really understand why Mary, the Mother of the Bridegroom as well as the Bride, and the Apostles, Christ's servants and dispensers of the secrets of God, had to be present in Cana. To the greatest joys of the priesthood belongs the revealing and furthering of the wonderful secret of Christianity, the relationship between the Bridegroom and Bride, between Christ and His Christian people, between Jesus and the individual soul. In this sense let us think about this marriage day in Cana.

It should be emphasized from the beginning that what will be said about Bride and Groom are not just poetical images, but rather fundamental truths of the Christian faith, basic facts and laws of the world of the supernatural. Jesus is the Bridegroom. Jesus as Bridegroom is Head of the Church, as the man is head of the woman (Eph. 5:23). Bridegroom and Bride, Head and Body, Christ and Church remain an inseparable unity, two who are actually one! One cannot talk of the one without at the same time thinking of the other. One cannot talk about a body without thinking about the head, of a bride without a bridegroom, of the King without His Queen, of the Church without remembering Jesus. The Bride is only a bride insofar as she has a bridegroom. The body lives only insofar as it is joined to the head. One speaks of the Queen only because she belongs to the King. The Church exists only because and insofar as she is dependent on Jesus.

Every other society may continue to exist independent of its founder, more or less well, for a shorter or a longer period, on the basis of the vitality it possesses, just as a child, once it has come into the world, can continue to exist even without its mother. This does not apply to the Church. The Church is a supernatural society and therefore possesses no life independent of her Founder. She lives and moves and has her being exclusively in Jesus. Jesus is the life of the Church. Everything that is done by the Church is done by Jesus. When the Church baptizes, it is Jesus Who baptizes. When the Church confirms, it is Jesus Who confirms. When the Church sacrifices and transubstantiates, it is Jesus Who sacrifices and transubstantiates. When the Church absolves, it is Jesus Who absolves. When the Church blesses, it is Jesus Who blesses. When the

Church prays, it is Jesus Who prays. The King does everything through the Queen.

The priest, the bishop or the pope is only a representative, an organ of the living and acting Christ. Certainly he is a necessary organ, but nevertheless only an organ, a member, a tool. Jesus comes into the life of the Church as lifegiving, moving Principle who is so much in the foreground that the Church is referred to as Christ living on. Just as in marriage the family name of the bride gives way to the husband's name, so in the history of the Church, which began on Pentecost, which was both the birthday and the wedding day of the Church, the name and the work of the Bride must recede into the background, giving place to those of the King. The Bride and the children of the Bride must bear the name of the Bridegroom Jesus. All other names, if they do not disappear, must give Him pride of place. The Personality and the Name before which all knees must bend is the Name Jesus! Jesus is all in all for Church history.

Whatever else is great and worthy and holy, was and is so only insofar as it comes from Jesus. It must be a member of his Mystical Body, the Church, which is flooded with divine life. We know that the Church serves no idols in its saints. Basically the Bride knows only her Bridegroom Jesus. It is impossible to have a more wonderful and more universal concept of the place of Christ in Christianity than the Catholic Church has always had since the days of the Apostles and the ancient Church Fathers. The Church wants only to be Christ living on! That is the great mystery of which St. Paul repeatedly speaks in his epistles: Jesus cares for the Christians as for His own Body. The Christians are members in Christ. The Christians are something of Jesus.

If one learns to know the King, one also becomes acquainted with the Queen. If Jesus is the life principle of the Church, so much that all supernatural actions of the body and the members, the Church and the Christians may and must be regarded also as His actions, then the task of the Church consists singularly and exclusively in binding herself most devotedly to Christ her Head. There is no warning which St. Paul writes more urgently or more often in his letters than to be and live *in Christo Jesu*, in Christ Jesus. The same applies to the writings of St. John.

In the course of the centuries and particularly in more recent times, a rich number of devotions and religious exercises have been introduced for the purpose of renewing the faithful. In practice, however, all these devotions and exercises are only as useful as the amount to which they further the queen of all devotions and exercises, the union of the individual soul with Jesus. The union of the soul with Jesus is the real vital question in the supernatural world order, whether we are speaking of those in the purgative, illuminative or unitive states. We only fulfill our God-willed functions as members of Christ to the extent that our union with the Head has been established. On the other hand, we are ill, lame or dead to the extent that the connection of the member with the Head is disturbed, suspended or destroyed.

This ongoing union of the member with the Head of the Christians, with Christ the King, is threefold. First, it is a union of the member with the Head as supernatural Source of Life. We are Christians not only in name, but in the full sense of the world. We are adopted children of God, bearers of supernatural, divine life, only through Jesus the Head. We speak of means of grace, of sacraments, and rightly so. But above the seven sacraments stands the sacrament, above the seven streams of grace the Source of Grace, above the various means of grace the actual, great, personal, divine Means of Grace, Christ Jesus the King.

The second is the union with the Head as supernatural Source of Light. In the head is the eye; in the head is thought. The hand is *per se* a blind organ. The hand alone does not know what it ought to do. In all things it must follows its head. The Head which the hand of the Christian must follow is Jesus. To be a Christian means to regard everything in the light of faith in Jesus, the Light of the World, not in the mere reflected light of natural understanding.

The third is the union with the Head as supernatural Source of Power. The member, let's say for example the hand, does not move of its own accord. It only moves because the head moves it, and it moves however the head moves it by means of the nerves and muscles. In the supernatural order it is no different. All actions of a Christian should not only be taken because he wants to do them, but because Jesus wills them and however Jesus wills them. All movements initiated only by the hand and not by the Head, thus originating from purely natural and not supernatural motivations, done not for God's sake, even though done with so-called good intentions, are without supernatural merit in God's sight and are worthless for eternity. They are not rooted in Christ Jesus!

And that is the great evil of our naturalist, modernist times! The hand acts alone. We are very busy in all sorts of fields. Yet the hands of the Christians are not usually moved by the Head, not by Jesus, but rather by nature, the spirit of the times, our own stubbornness, our own will, our own interests. Our activities, especially our public ones, our economic, political and everyday doings and comings and goings do not really live in Jesus anymore. The relationship with the King is missing.

The People of God—a frequent concept in the Old Testament—looks to others and runs after others. Seized by the modern spirit, it follows adulterous ways. It is thinking of separation and divorce. Christ and Christendom belong together as an indissoluble union like head and body. That is the meaning of the motto of Pope St. Pius X: "Restore all things in Christ." The Bride, Christendom, should return to her Bridegroom. She should combat all liberal and modern desires to commit adultery, all flirting the world. Whatever she does, whether eating and drinking or anything else, however she works, amuses herself, buys or sells, writes or talks, makes politics or prays, her entire day's activities should be in Jesus! The Bride belongs to the Bridegroom. That and that alone is Christianity! Back to the King!

THE HOUSE OF THE KING

The Catholic church is the house of the King. The Catholic church is built for the choir, the choir is built for the Tabernacle holding the ciborium, the ciborium is made for the most holy Sacrament. All arts serve the King in the Host: architecture, sculpture, painting and music.

As soon as the sacred Host disappears, the church becomes architectural nonsense. If the King is not there, it is no longer necessary to build churches, but only the most practical of meeting halls. That is why Protestant architecture has been on the wrong track for most of the past four hundred years. It has built as though the King were still there; it has ordered the building toward a tabernacle (which in reality is no longer there) instead of building only for the pulpit.

The Catholic religion is the religion of Christ Present. Not all Catholics are aware of this truth. Many of them see only the gigantic structure of a system of thought towering to the heavens, before which all systems of the philosophers are nothing but clay huts, shacks and barracks. Others see in Catholicism only the beautiful morality. They look at Catholicism only from the vantage point of the street or at best the main entrance.

Whoever really wants to become acquainted with Catholicism in its innermost essence must go further up front, up to the tabernacle where Jesus is. His Catholicism must become Eucharistic, it must think and act Eucharistically. Catholicism without the living center in the sacred Host is dead, soulless Catholicism.

The Catholic Church is the dwelling of the sacred Host! What does that mean? Christ never spoke more clearly than when He spoke of the most holy Sacrament. A year before His death, following the miraculous multiplication of the loaves of bread, He preached in the synagogue of Capharnaum and said, despite the resistance of the people and the greater part of His disciples: "My flesh is meat indeed" (Jn. 6:56). And a year later, on the day before His death, He said with a clarity that brooked no objections, after He had taken the bread into His hands and blessed it: "This is my body."

He commanded and empowered His Apostles and their rightful successors with the words: "Do this in remembrance of me," to do the same that He had done, namely to bless wine and bread, to consecrate them that they become His Body and His Blood, and to receive them as food for the soul. Where Christ's living Body is, there is also His Blood and His Soul, for there can be no living body without both. And where Christ's Humanity is, there also is His Godhood, for the one is inseparable from the other in one Person.

The sentence is therefore valid: Wherever the Host is, there also is Jesus. Thus the Catholic church as the dwelling of the sacred Host is the dwelling of Jesus. Jesus lives here, truly, really, essentially. He is not listed in the telephone book, but in the Gospel it is an undeniable truth.

The Catholic Church, the house of the sacred Host! Let's think about this further. Let's penetrate the veil of the outer form of bread to Him Who is hidden under it. Christ Present in the Sacrament is not a dead person, but rather a living Person. The tabernacle is not a coffin, not a place where someone is asleep, and the choir of the church building is no cemetery! Nowhere in the world is there more life than here. Nowhere is more work being done.

What Christ once said after the healing of the man who had been sick for 38 years applies also to the Eucharistic Savior: "My Father worketh unto now; and I work" (Jn. 5:17). In the tabernacle lives Omnipotence. In the tabernacle lives endless Love. In the tabernacle lives the eternal Wisdom. In the tabernacle lives divine Providence. From here the souls are guided. From here flow out the streams of life. Here the King works.

Here is the real parish office. From here the angels of the parish receive their orders and commands. Here they submit their reports. Excuse the military expression, but here is the office of the General Staff, where the great Silent One works out the mobilization, attack and defence plans for the spiritual battles of His Church. Here is the King's residence.

We are blind. Our spiritual sight takes in only the surface of things. If God would open our eyes, we would see a whole world in the sacred Host, a world of miracles, a heaven full of life, light and power, full of beauty and consolation, flowing into all the alleyways, into all minds, all hearts. That is the truth of the tabernacle. The tabernacle is the paradise planted upon earth—not the visible, but the far more precious, higher paradise of supernatural life.

The Catholic church is the place where Jesus dwells! What follows from that? longing for the Invisible One in our tabernacles, for the Eucharistic paradise of the Catholic churches! Jesus is the Center of Creation. Everything must strive toward Jesus. Everything must be drawn by the holy Host: understanding, fantasy, will, memory, heart, even the body, the eyes, the ears, the feet, the hands, the tongue.

Everything must be oriented toward the Eucharist: think of Jesus, meditate Jesus, contemplate Jesus, want Jesus, go to Jesus, talk with Jesus. It is the fulfillment of those words spoken in Holy Week: I shall draw all things unto me. I shall reign! Thus can one recognize true Christianity in a Christian: The more our tabernacles and the Divine Heart of Jesus attract us like magnets, and the more we follow His pull, the more Christianity we have.

Make a Eucharistic examination of conscience. Is Jesus King of your mind? Is your mind Eucharistic? Does the sacred Host draw it like a magnet? Do you like to think about Jesus? Is your memory Eucharistic? Do you remember your own First Communion, do you think about your last Communion, about the eternal light? Is your imagination Eucharistic? When you are in Church, do you imagine Jesus as living and present?

Is Jesus King of your heart? Is your will Eucharistic? Do you burn with longing to receive Jesus again or to visit Him again? Are you hungry and thirsty for Jesus? Are your feet Eucharistic? Do you like to pay a short visit to the Holy of Holies on your way to or from work? Do you at least occasionally make the sacrifice of getting up earlier on a work day to attend Holy Mass? Are your eyes Eucharistic? Do you, like the saints, look only at the tabernacle and not bother about anything else? With what eyes do you regard the sacred Host and the chalice during the Consecration? Tell me whether you are Eucharistic and whether Christ is your King, and I will tell you whether you are Catholic.

The Catholic church is the house of the sacred Host! Jesus is our Teacher. It follows that the Catholic church is also a school, a school for all ages, all families, all states and walks of life, all levels of education. If the Catholic church is the official and obligatory school, then the best, most beautiful, most worthy of all teaching materials is the sacred Host. In a wonderful little Italian book is written, "All books written by human hands, even those written by the greatest saints, are not worth as much as this little white wafer, the sacred Host."

It is the book written within and without. On the inside it is written by the greatness of Jesus, on the outside by His humility and wondrous simplicity. It is the history of the eternal love of God for mankind, written by Jesus. This wonderful book, which one can never read to the end, should be our prayer book, our best meditation book, our "short catechism," our law book. Ask what Jesus would do or say in your case, and then you will know what you should do or say. Jesus is our Teacher! the Catholic church building, house of our sacred Host, is our school, our heavenly academy, as a holy soul of modern times has said.

When John the Baptist saw Jesus by the Jordan River, he said: "Behold the Lamb of God!" Two of his disciples "heard him speak, and they followed Jesus. And Jesus turning, and seeing them following him, saith to them: What seek you? Who said to him: Rabbi (which is to say, being interpreted, Master), where dwellest thou? He saith to them: Come and see. They came, and saw where He abode, and they stayed with him that day..." (Jn. 1:36-39).

Today we have seen where the King lives. The Catholic church is the house where Jesus makes His Home. We want to go and see and speak with Jesus. If people only knew what a joy it is to be with the King for even a quarter of an hour, and to speak with Him, then the churches would be filled day and night, and Jesus in the tabernacle would no longer be alone and forsaken. An hour at the foot of the tabernacle is worth more than a hundred years upon a throne. Come and see!

THE KING LIVES

For three years the twelve Apostles had the immeasurable joy of living in Jesus' company, of seeing and hearing Jesus. After the Resurrection the Apostles were prepared for a new way of the Lord's being present with them. Now Jesus no longer walked visibly among the people. He appeared only now and then miraculously in the circle of His faithful. From Ascension day until Judgment Day the visible presence of Christ is replaced by the invisible presence. Jesus in His divine wisdom found a means of being absent and present at the same time, absent for the eyes and ears, present for faith and the heart. This means is the Sacrament in the tabernacle.

The Apostles had difficulties in accustoming themselves to the invisible presence after three years of Jesus' visible company. That is why the Savior had to prepare them gently but earnestly for this following the first Holy Communion. "Yet a little while and ye shall see me no more," He said, "for I go to the Father!" Even among us Christians today there are few who would not prefer the visible presence of Jesus to His invisible presence. However, we must try and free ourselves from this quite natural view. The witness of faith must mean more to us than that of the eyes and ears. The main thing is that Jesus the King is here, not that He cannot be seen. The joy over His words, "I am with you even unto the end of the world," must prevail over the pain of the words, "Ye shall see me no more."

That we are vitally permeated with the actual presence of our King is characteristic of our religion. Catholicism is not merely a marvellous teaching, a wonderful moral system, an unexcelled organization. It is more. It is the real, living, present Jesus with His Mystical Body, *i.e.,* the faithful united with Him. It is not so much a theory as it is something living. A Catholicism that would not be united with Jesus would be nothing but a phantom in the mist, a soulless shell with another name and another outlook than its own.

That is why it is perhaps dangerous to faith if we use misunderstood words like Christianity and Catholicism somewhat too often. Let us repeat: Catholicism is not a theory, not a teaching. Christianity is the invisible but truly living presence of Christ among us, the Kingship of Jesus. To be Catholic means to stand in vital communication, through faith, hope and love, with the invisibly present Redeemer, the Way, the Truth, and the Life.

Thus it is that there, where Jesus is not present in the Host and no living communication with Him takes place, there can be no living Christianity. In that moment when Luther rejected the Sacrament of the Altar and therewith Christ present, he rejected Christianity.

Christianity equals Christ with the Christians! What does Jesus do when He is with the Christians? The same thing he did for three years in Palestine: be King. We often have no real concept of the life and the effectiveness of Jesus in the tabernacle. We think that because our eyes and ears are too weak to observe the divine-human activity of Jesus in the tabernacle, only the stillness of death reigns there. That is a gross deception.

His activity depends neither upon the greatness of his work room nor the loudness of sounds. What gigantic work is done by sun and nature, although no eye and no ear can observe its progress! The Jesus of the tabernacle is the same as the Jesus of the Gospels, the same in Holiness, in Might, in Wisdom, in Omniscience, in Mercy and in Love. St. Paul writes in Hebrews (13:8) that "Jesus Christ, yesterday, and to-day; and the same for ever."

So what is Jesus doing in the tabernacles? He exercises His priestly office. The King prays. He holds perpetual adoration. He holds services in the name of the parish. He celebrates the Holy Mass. The visible Mass is over with the *Ite missa est*. The invisible Mass continues day and night since Jesus is present in the tabernacle, as an offering of praise and thanks and reparation. The parish priest is obliged by canon law to "read" Holy Mass for the congregation every Sunday. That is called "application." Jesus does more than the visible priest. He prays and makes application for His people continually.

What else does Jesus do in the tabernacle? He exercises His office as Shepherd. He does pastoral care of souls. The King keeps watch. The eyes of the Good Shepherd never sleep. They see everything that happens in the parish, in the houses and in the hearts. The eyes of the Good Shepherd take note of every longing for help and every danger. The Heart of the Good Shepherd beats for all with unending love, and that is the soul of pastoral work.

What else does Jesus do in the tabernacle? He exercises the preaching office, a preaching that penetrates deeper than just to the ears and without which the preaching of the clergy in the pulpit remains nothing but sounding brass and tinkling cymbal. The King speaks. The angels are His parish helpers. They visit the individual souls of the parishioners on assignment from the Savior and with the power of the Holy Spirit. That proves what ought to be proven: that Christianity is no empty theory. Christianity is Christ with the Christians! The King lives!

From the reverse standpoint we come to the same result: Christianity is the Christian with Christ. The value of the Christianity of Christians is directly proportional to the amount of personal relationship with Christ in the individual person. Thus it was with the Apostles. The Personality of Jesus was everything to them. Their dogmatic theology was Jesus. Their moral theology was Jesus. Their ascesis was Jesus. Their pastoral theology was Jesus. Their canon law was Jesus. Their whole theology, the whole sum of their knowledge was Jesus. They did not study science for three years, but rather they studied Jesus for three years. Therefore we can well understand why it was endlessly hard for them not to hear and see Him anymore.

Christianity should not be anything else for us than it was for the Apostles: a living relationship to Jesus present. This personal relationship expresses itself as faith, hope and love for Jesus the King. Above all it is the Christian with Christ through love! Take for example in thought. Love expresses itself in its domination of the entire world of our thoughts. The world of thoughts usually is preoccupied with business, pleasure, the latest sensation, exaggerated worries and often just dirt. It is materialistic, money-grabbing, sensual, alcoholic, worldly. It is the thought of a baptized heathen. If we want to call ourselves Christians, then we ought to think of nothing but Christ Who is present among us. Neither work nor politics, neither the press nor science nor sports ought to occupy us in the least in comparison to the occupation of our memory and our understanding by Jesus. That's Christianity!

The same applies to the world of feelings. Measure your temperature in Church, near to Jesus. It is much lower than when you are in a theater, a restaurant, in the office. That's not normal. You must have a heart defect. And today it seems that cardiac defects have become the mass epidemic of Christianity. We love everything, only not Jesus. I repeat: that's not normal! A patient whose temperature has sunk so low is very ill. Christianity is the Christian with Christ. Not only with his thoughts and his feelings, but in all his doings must he be with Him. The church, the house where Jesus lives, ought to be a stronger attraction for every genuine Christian than any other house in town, even during the week. Tell me where I can find you most often, and I'll tell you what you are.

We want to be Christians again! Yet a little while, and we shall see Jesus. The Invisible will become visible. The hidden King of the tabernacle is Judge over punishment or reward for eternity! The great moment of decision over heaven and hell has come. What is heaven? The place of blessed happiness in love. It is clear that whoever does not know the great law of Christianity, the law of love between the Christian and Christ, cannot enter into heaven. Not to want to love Christ, Who is Love, is the sin of sins! Whoever does not love will be damned. We want to become Christians again. We want to love again, love and die for Christ the King.

UNDER THE EYES OF THE KING

There are priests who live in a spiritual wilderness. When they sow, they sow on stony earth. Nothing grows. Everything seems to be in vain. But Jesus once said to a soul: "When a priest can do nothing more, then there remains only one thing for him. He must become a saint." The life of the saints is full of conversions. What Jesus said to the priests applies to all. When their good works fall on hard, fruitless soil, then they must become saints.

Is it any use to speak of holiness in front of everybody, is not the vocation of most people filled with so much work and worry that there can be no mention of striving for perfection? The answer is simple: God wills it. What we shall one day be in eternity, if we do not want to be damned, that we must strive to be on earth. We have no right to except the common folk from this rule. If we ask little from people, then even that little will not be worth much. If we want people to become much, then we have to demand much of them. The phrase, "Not everyone is called to be a saint," is, as a modern author has rightly said, a demonic phrase. It comes from the devil. It draws mankind down into the depths. Whoever doesn't want to be what God's holy will for him is, runs the risk of becoming nothing.

The canonization of St. Therese of the Child Jesus surely was intended, among other things, to counter the opinion that one needs extraordinary means to achieve holiness. Neither the number nor the length of religious exercises makes for holiness, but rather the strength of our love. Without exaggeration we can say: Jesus dwells in my soul. Believe this, act accordingly, and you will become holy. Companionship with Jesus Who lives in you is a principal means of perfection.

Be for the King dwelling in your soul a golden censer of perpetual adoration. Sacrifice to Him the sweet-scented smoke clouds of your reverence, your thanks, your love, day and night. To this purpose think often of His divine presence within you. Do not forget Him. Stay with Him. Do not look for unnecessary diversions. Never let Jesus alone. I have read about a small boy who had this basic principle: "I must always be at home. I must never go out completely." The reason for this extraordinary wisdom in a child was that the boy knew that Jesus was at home within him. And when Jesus is at home, one must not go out completely. Granted, you have to fulfill the duties of your vocation or profession, you ought to work, you should be friendly to your fellow men and women, and you should also occasionally relax.

But you ought to arrange work, companionship and amusement so that you never go too far away from Jesus. We must do everything under the eyes of the King. We must not lose sight of Jesus. Jesus and the soul should be able to say a word to one another and hear each other now and again in the middle of whatever we are doing. Above all, we must not run away from Jesus in order to indulge in useless and superfluous thoughts, memories, worries, plans, conversations and amusements. Every honest examination of conscience each evening proves that we have failed a hundred times during the day through such distractions, through unnecessary visits of the soul away from home, through superfluous external activities, through too much chatting under the window and outside the door, thus turning our backs on Jesus unnecessarily, wasting minutes and seconds and perhaps even quarters of an hour, which we could have spent at the feet of the Lord, despite all our work. Do not forget the censer, the good intention, the glance at your Jesus Who dwells within you. Make your whole day into a church service. You can do it!

Be a pure tabernacle to the King dwelling within you. For the Holiest of Holies only the holy is good enough. The priests of the Old and the New Covenants are to serve the Most High with golden vessels. Trembling in holy reverence, the angels sing their eternal *Sanctus* before the All-Holy, for fear that something imperfect might be found in them. For heaven tolerates nothing unclean. The thought, "Jesus the All-Holy in me," should purge away all dross on the soul like a burning fire. A vessel must be suited to its content, the dwelling to its Guest. As Jesus, so must you be! Don't forget yourself! Think of who you are! Don't throw yourself away! Don't make yourself mean!

Pure be your head, with no vain towering hairdo and golden barettes! Pure be your eye, pure your ear, pure your tongue. Have no base curiosity, no loveless insults to others, no uncouth words! Pure be your clothing, no compromises with provocative fashion!

Pure be your morality. Have nothing to do with that which makes men lower than animals, nothing which destroys mutual respect! Pure be the world of your thoughts! No selfishness, no self-adoration! You are a tabernacle. In you dwells Jesus! If you have committed a fault, purify your tabernacle with an act of complete remorse or through a worthy confession. With the grace of the Holy Ghost, renew your soul as though it were a church being dedicated. Become once again a tabernacle with body and soul!

Be a monstrance for the King dwelling within you! Let Jesus shine through the veil of your poor human nature. Be with your life a continuous exposition of the Most Blessed. Who sees you should see Jesus. Of course your appearance will remain yours, but your behavior be that of Jesus. Who hears you should hear Jesus. They will recognize your voice as your own, but the tone should be that of Jesus. Whoever keeps company with you should feel Jesus' nearness. Outwardly they will notice nothing unusual, nothing special, nothing peculiar, just an ordinary person. But whoever listens attentively should sense the heartbeat of the Divine Heart of Jesus in you.

There are those people we meet in life that we call doubles. They are so similar to one another that one can hardly tell them apart. We ought all to become such doubles of Jesus. According to the teaching of St. Paul: "And I live, now not I; but Christ liveth in me" (Gal. 2:20). Jesus within, therefore Jesus outside as well! The true Christian should be a monstrance of Christ and an uninterrupted exposition of the Most Holy! There you have your assignment. You must show Jesus within you to your environment and live Jesus in you for others.

Once the Savior said to a soul: "I have been your Tenant for more than eight years. Haven't I paid the rent well?" That is the King of our hearts. First He gives us the unspeakable joy of being our Guest, and then He rewards us in addition, if we make the poor stable of our heart available to Him. Jesus will do the same for you. If you make His visit in your soul pleasant, He will not fail to pay you rent. He will bless your house and your hearth. He will raise and protect your loved ones through His Holy Spirit. So loving and good is Jesus!

THE KING'S BANQUET

If the Church, in accordance with the teaching of St. Paul, is the Mystical Body of Christ, then she must have a head and a heart like any other body. Jesus is her Head and Heart. The Head works mainly in Rome, the Heart in the tabernacle. The Head reveals itself especially in the Holy Father, the Heart in the Eucharist. Both are vital necessities. If the head and the heart no longer work, the body dies. If Catholicism were no longer papal and Eucharistic, it would cease to exist.

Whoever says "pope" and "tabernacle," says Jesus Christ, because the papacy and the sacrament of the altar are the two great channels through which Jesus Christ rules the world. And whoever says the word Jesus Christ, the Word before Whom everything must bow in heaven, on earth and under the earth, has said everything. The Name of Jesus is the answer to all problems, all secrets, all difficulties.

If we have the pope and the Eucharist, the Head and the Heart, why is the Body so ill? Although we receive Holy Communion, why are we not better, purer, more willing to sacrifice, more patient, more humble? This question is very apt in a time of frequent Communions. What's wrong?

What is Communion? What should it be? Communion is union. What is union? Union presupposes two who desire to be one. Where there is only one, there can be no talk of communion. Where there are two, but two who pass by one another without speaking, there can also be no talk of communion. Communion is two that equal one.

Who are the two? Jesus and you. That is Communion: Jesus and you. It must be said in that order, Jesus and you, not you and Jesus. In Communion everything depends upon who is first and who is second, who stands in the foreground and who is in the background, who is the star and who is the extra. In the Communion of the lukewarm souls, the *ego* is in the foreground and Jesus in the background; in the Communion of the devoted souls, Jesus is in the foreground and the *ego* in the background. Jesus reigns.

In other words, preparation and disposition are of vital importance for Communion. It is true that the sacrament is effective of itself, but only insofar as no hurdles are placed in its way. It is the same with light: light shines in the darkness, but if something is hung before the rays of light or if we close our eyes, the light's effect is blocked.

It is also like nutrition. It is not just a matter of eating healthy and strengthening food. Our digestive system must also possess the capacity of digesting the food we eat. Otherwise eating is useless. Therefore: the effectiveness of the sacrament depends upon the ability of the recipient to take it in, *i.e.,* according to the disposition. And here we have the reason why the results of Holy Communion are so lacking in some people. They have a lack of good disposition.

Why cannot Jesus develop His work in the soul? Perhaps because there is no room? The question of room plays just as fatal a role in Communion as it did in Bethlehem. The minds and hearts are often full of alien things, superfluous matters, miscellaneous, vain, worldly, dangerous, even sinful or evil thoughts. They are full of the world and of the self, whether in the category of "worldly" the problem is materialism, addiction to amusement or sensuality, and whether that of "self" applies to arrogance, vanity or self-right-eousness. Such people apparently want Jesus to come to them, but not that He should reign in them.

The fact is that modern man lives from Sunday to Saturday, from the first to the last year of his life in a world which is alien to the tabernacle. And now, take this modern person, who breaths the air of a completely foreign atmosphere, and set him into the atmosphere of the supernatural that surrounds the altar. What happens? He's there with his body. He communicates with his tongue. But that is no real union. It is not soul-to-soul, spirit-to-spirit and heart-to-heart. Jesus comes, as it were, into the front yard of the soul. Figuratively speaking, one only says hello at the front door.

This person says a few pious words, which he calls Communion prayers, but he doesn't let Jesus into the most intimate shrine of his soul. He does not talk personally about his most intimate secrets. He has not led Jesus to the throne, but instead dealt with Him quickly like a beggar or an unwelcome guest. Then he turns his back and goes to the window to chat with Mrs. World, as though he actually were not at home, and every couple of minutes he looks at his wristwatch to see whether the official 15-minute reception hour is soon over. That is how people often do it. That is how we often treat the King. We have no room and no time for Jesus. We communicate without communicating. That is why we don't come back from the Communion rail as saints, but instead like the same people we were before.

What ought Communion to be? The opposite of that which we just described. It should be Jesus at the center of the soul and the *ego* at His feet. In other words, Jesus as Lord of the House, and the "old man" outside the door. Fr. Ravignan once quoted someone: "You ask me what I did during my novitiate? I answer: We were two. I threw one of us out of the window, and now I am alone." Communion should be an enthronement!

What is the precondition for such a Communion? First of all, strong faith. If one should not begin to pray at all without first evoking a living act of faith in the presence of God, with Whom one wants to converse, then how much more does this apply to the first quarter hour after the Holy Communion! I must be saturated with the thought that Jesus is there, Jesus, the Son of the Living God, Jesus, Son of Man, Jesus my King. I must say that to myself again and again, because I am forgetful and superficial. Forgetful and superficial people need always to be reminded of the same thing.

Let us imagine that the Blessed Virgin Mary would honor us with a visit every day and talk with us for a quarter of an hour. A Communion is more than such a vision. It is more important than the visit of all the angels and saints. But I must be filled with this faith to my deepest depths. I must believe it: Jesus is there! Otherwise our whole Communion devotion, our whole thanksgiving, remains cold and dry.

The thought of Jesus must work in us like sunrise, like the beginning of a new day. The physical world disappears, and the one which now appears is the world of grace, the world of the Divine Heart, much more rich and beautiful than all that human eyes see and human ears hear.

How can I attempt to paint and describe this world of grace? I have not the colors, I have not the words. You cannot paint Jesus, you cannot describe Him. Jesus is too beautiful. A saintly soul has said: "If the world could behold Jesus, as I have seen Him, then all souls would be absorbed in such a sight, leave their businesses, the pleasures, their politics, and, ravished by the sight of the King of Glory and Love, see nothing more than Him and worship Him alone."

You do not see this Jesus. But once more I say: the important thing is not that you see Him, but rather that He is there and that you believe. Jesus is there, in me, in the midst of my heart, as King. Then you can pray. Then you can wonder. Then you can love. Then you can cry and mourn. And all that even without the prayer book! And 15 minutes will seem too short to you, the most beautiful minutes of your day and your week. When you come home, you will be purer, calmer, friendlier to your fellow men, more compassionate and more humble.

Let us not make the precious time after Holy Communion so complicated, so difficult, so unnatural. Let us think of only one thing: Jesus is there. Everything else comes of its own accord. And if afterward someone should ask you what you did, then say: A great deal, but actually only one thing. For 15 minutes I have believed, hoped and loved! That is Communion! Jesus and you! Jesus in the center of your soul! Jesus as King. Come and see how sweet the Lord is. But come alone. Leave the world outside the doors. If you finally understand the right way to go to receive Holy Communion, you will also soon understand the right way to live.

THE KING OF HEARTS

Even though I am Swiss, it is not the mountains and lakes, not the cities and villages of my homeland that interest me most, but rather a little round Something that lives in our tabernacles and of which my faith tells me: That is Jesus, the One through Whom the people, the mountains, the lakes, the meadows and the forests were made, and without Whom was made nothing that was made.

That which is the Center of all things should forever remain the Center, and that means for the citizen and the statesman as well. There is a saying: "All roads lead to Rome." There is a law of the spiritual life which decrees: All roads lead to Jesus. The various devotions are only of value insofar as they are ways toward Jesus, whether it be the holy Mass, the reception of the sacraments, meditation, the practice of the presence of God, spiritual reading or the examination of conscience.

The most important fact of our religious life is Jesus, King of the heart. Jesus can be King in us by various ways and means. He is mystically present in the members of the Church. Through Baptism we are made members of the Mystical Body of Christ, which we call the Church. All the faithful are, according to the teaching of Holy Scripture, one body and one Spirit under the Head, which is Christ (Eph. 4).

It is impossible to express more clearly the togetherness and the common life of Christ and the Christian. It is impossible to be a closer neighbor than Head and member are to one another. The neighborliness between the Christian and Christ is so immediate that they become one, in a certain sense. St. Augustine rejoiced: "Let us congratulate one another! We have not only become Christians, but Christ." The Head and the members are together the whole Christ. He and us! I announce to you tidings of great joy: If you are a Christian, then Christ is in you as Head and King.

Following the first Holy Communion Jesus used yet another parable: "I am the Vine; you the branches. As the branch cannot bear fruit in itself, unless it abide in the vine, so neither can you, unless you abide in me" (Jn. 15:5,4). Jesus never exaggerates. Every exaggeration would be a lie, and Jesus is the Truth. If Jesus says something, then it is so, no matter how unbelievable it may seem. If you are Catholic, if you are a branch of the Vine which is Christ, then there can be no closer relationship or neighborliness than between you and Jesus. It is not enough to say: Jesus is with you. Jesus is in you. Rejoice and be glad!

But all that does not seem to be enough for Jesus. The teaching of the Head and the member, the Vine and the branch, does not yet completely express the reign of Christ over you. Listen, Jesus says even more: If anyone love me, he will keep My word, and I will come to him and make My abode with him. And I will manifest Myself to him (*Cf.* Jn. 14:23, 21). That is why St. Paul in his epistles repeatedly calls the Christians temples of the Holy God (*cf.* II Cor. 6:16; I Cor. 3:16). God lives in them and they live in God.

God is the measureless temple of their souls and their souls are the temple of the measureless God, the palace of the King.

The Eternal One seems to forget Who He is and who the human being is, in order to be able to bring about an incomprehensible miracle of love. Yet this miracle is the great fact of Christianity. It is the dogma on which the teaching of the supernatural dignity of the Christian as adoptive child of God is based. It causes the soul in the state of grace to be of more worth than the whole visible creation, all the goods and glories of the earth.

The mightiest and most beautiful cathedral is in the last analysis only made of perishable materials. You are more. You are "partakers of the divine nature," as St. Peter wrote (II Pet. 1:4), God the Holy One lives in you. Thus does Jesus also live in you, even when the sacred Humanity of Our Lord is no longer sacramentally present in you. Because the Son of God is also the Son of Man, because there is no Son of God Who is not at the same time a partaker of human nature, we can and may claim at any time, even outside the time of Holy Communion when the form of the bread is no longer present in us: Jesus is in you. You are a living Church of Christ, the palace of the King.

There is more to come! That which we have heard up to now is so great that if it were everything, then you might perhaps be able to envy the tabernacle, because Jesus abides in the tabernacle day and night, also in His sacred Humanity. The tabernacle thus appears to be richer than your heart. The reply to that is that your soul in a state of grace is more valuable than the most beautiful tabernacle and the most precious ciborium in the world. The tabernacle and the ciborium are things of the dust of earth, but your soul is a partaker of the divine nature.

Therefore the tabernacle is not the end of the line. It is only the next to last stop for the Eucharistic Savior. You are the last station. Christ did not institute the Most Blessed Sacrament primarily for the tabernacle's sake, but for the sake of you heart. Jesus wants to be King of your Heart. Jesus is homesick for your soul, the living tabernacle. We often find among devoted Christians an actual hunger and thirst for the Holy Communion. This hunger for the Holy Communion, for union, is much stronger in Jesus than in the saint. It is endless because His love is endless.

It can even go so far as to bring about a miracle. We read in the lives of especially privileged souls that the Redeemer not only remained present in them for a short quarter of an hour, but even for several hours, perhaps even from one Communion to the next. There is even no lack of those who say that in our extraordinary and so serious time Jesus repeats this miracle often. Whoever knows Jesus cannot hold this extraordinary lasting dwelling of the sacred Humanity of Jesus in the soul to be impossible. For Jesus is endlessly good and loving. All in all: The great fact of Christianity is Jesus in the soul of the Christian, Jesus King of Hearts.

An eternal light belongs in front of the tabernacle. Therefore, if you are a tabernacle in which the Son of the Living God truly lives and dwells, then you must not forget the eternal light. The eternal light that should burn day and night before your living tabernacle is love: conscious, strong, vital, lasting love. This eternal light of love for Christ should always burn and never be extinguished, not even out on the street, in the workshop or in the office. Even when the winds of temptation blow, they must not blow it out. Here especially it must burn brightly. Not even in the Gethsemane hours may it die out. Therefore let the continually repeated short prayer of your life and the favorite prayer of your heart be this greeting to Jesus abiding in you: My Jesus, my all! Jesus King of my heart!

ENTHRONED IN THE FAMILY

I like to think about the royal official of Capharnaum. This man pleases me, not only because of what one can read between the lines. He believed. That was not enough for him. He immediately made his faith the law of his house. He regarded himself as the responsible king and lawgiver in his little kingdom.

There are many kings and governments, but few really understand how to rule. That includes the kingdom of the family! Most home governments are liberal: every member does what he pleases. At least in Catholic families, this is unfortunately often the case. They frequently have the weakest house government. A Protestant or a socialist husband is more likely to have a strict regime at home. His Catholic wife may plead and argue with the greatest justification, but he likes to declare: I am the man! And then he returns to business as usual.

When I think of that manly figure in Capharnaum, then I feel a deep longing for strong Catholic men and self-confident, strong, Catholic family rulers who, without being tyrants, understand how to form the whole house according to their faith and their will.

How can we get back to truly Catholic family government like in the good old days? In our century an apostle travelled throughout the world like a conqueror. His name was Fr. Mateo, and he belonged to the Congregation of the Most Sacred Heart. His home was Peru in South America. In the French shrine of the Sacred Heart of Jesus in Paray-le-Monial he was cured instantly of a mortal illness, though all the doctors had given up on him. Thereafter he went preaching and conquering through the countries of Latin America, the United States, Canada, Spain, France, Holland, Italy. Miracles of grace accompanied him.

What did this man want? He declared: The misery of the world begins in the family! The family, our first bulwark, has fallen. The family has been de-Christianized and secularized. It must become once again a supernatural institution, a domain of faith, love and grace. From the renewal of the family will follow as a matter of course the renewal of human society and of the state. Healing comes from the inside to the outside, just as illness begins internally and manifests itself externally. All physicians who only want to cure the family with external means instead of with a complete spiritual transfusion only cause a fiasco.

How can we come back to true Catholic family spirit? One can apply various means. In the Catholic Church there is no single "devotion" that is the exclusive means to salvation. However, according to Fr. Mateo one of the surest and fastest means is the enthronement of the Most Sacred Heart of Jesus in the family. Is that something new? No, something old! An American invention? No, an oriental invention that comes from Palestine, a divine invention, an invention from Bethlehem and Nazareth and Golgotha!

The enthronement of the Most Sacred Heart of Jesus is the literal representation of the sentence: "He believed and his whole house with him" (Jn. 4:53). The enthronement is a purely religious family feast. It is more important than many days in the history of the family, perhaps even more than the father's or the mother's name day or another anniversary, even as important as a Church feast, even perhaps Christmas or New Year. The whole family is together. Family members who are far away show with a letter that they are at least present in spirit. If possible, a priest comes to the home. All gather in the living room or main room of the house. In the most beautiful point in the home a picture or statue of the Sacred Heart of Jesus, blessed by the priest, is set in place by the head of the family and surrounded by flowers and lights. The whole family kneels, prays the Creed and consecrates itself to the Savior Who has been enthroned. The day will be commemorated in all years to come as a holy day on which all receive the Most Blessed Sacrament. The place of the enthronement is from then on the family shrine, where all important events in the family are hallowed.

Jesus enthroned by the family! Jesus King and Center of all who dwell in the house! What does that mean? We hate all empty ceremonies. God is Spirit, and must be worshipped in spirit and in truth. Every external ceremony has only one purpose: to sink a great thought deep into the soul of the onlookers and listeners. What does the enthronement of the Sacred Heard of Jesus preach to us? First of all the reign of love: God is love. Christianity is the religion of love.

When this is said, people usually think only of the love between human beings. They talk as though the first and noblest commandment did not exist. Christianity is primarily the religion of the love of God for mankind and the love of mankind for God. Thus it is written: "Thou shalt love the Lord thy God with thy whole heart, and with thy whole soul, and with thy whole strength" (Deut. 6:5). The misery of our modern Christianity is that we are so unutterably cold, so endlessly sober that we lack the soul of Christendom, the heart, the love and therewith the main thing. "He that loveth not, knoweth not God" (I Jn. 4:8).

Whoever does not know God is no Christian. His Christian name is robbery. What is the best illustration of the soul of Christianity, of God's love? Three things: the Cross, the Most Blessed Sacrament and the image of the Sacred Heart of Jesus. They are three preachers, all saying the same thing! However, because people no longer understood the first and the second sermon, God gave us the third, the image of the Sacred Heart, surrounded by flames, over it the Cross, girded by thorns, the eternal sermon: God is love. "By this hath the charity of God appeared towards us, because God hath sent his only begotten Son into the world, that we may live by him" (I Jn. 4:9). Whoever does not understand this language and cannot understand the picture of the Sacred Heart, is a hopeless case.

There is only one thing for us to do: We have to listen to this sermon. We should immerse ourselves often in this picture, transfixed and enraptured. We should expose ourselves to the rays of this divine fire, until we ourselves become warm. From childhood on, in good and in hard times, we should look into these eyes. We must pray unceasingly for this great grace: Sweet Heart of Jesus, grant that I may love Thee ever more and more. The Divine Heart of Jesus gives back to the family living room that temperature of love, without which no true family happiness and family peace can flourish.

Jesus enthroned in the family! That is a sermon on the reign of the Spirit of Jesus over our minds! Jesus is King. He said it Himself: "I am a King. For this came I into the world." The purpose of the enthronement is the reign of Jesus. He reigns alone! Christ cannot bear that Satan sit next to Him as co-regent on the throne, as though legally His spiritual equal. Only one can sit upon the throne: Christ!

The result is a gradual, complete transformation of family life. One pagan idol after the other will be carried out of the house, because it no longer fits in. The walls become cleaner. The library will be cleaned out. No periodicals by enemies of the Church lie on the family table anymore. Superfluous luxury and addiction to pleasures will disappear. Blasphemies and cursewords will no longer be heard. Work will become divine service. The whole house will become an island of peace! The picture of the Heart of Jesus will have become the reformer of family life.

Not only that! By singing *hosannas* to His special triumph on its knees, the little society of the family prepares the public enthronement of the Savior. The Divine Heart of Jesus has a policy of conquest. It wants to get out on the street. It wants to renew all of public life. As soon as it becomes the reformer of the family, it wants to become the reformer of human society. The petition in the Our Father should become reality: Thy kingdom come! Thy will be done on earth as it is in heaven! Hallowed be Thy name! Whoever promotes the enthronement of the Sacred Heart of Jesus in the family becomes active for the cause of human society itself. He becomes a benefactor of humankind.

A person who has become acquainted with the Divine Heart of Christ in a family cannot remain silent. He will be compelled to tell about his happiness. He will also communicate it to others. He will become an apostle. That is what we need! We have become so terribly reticent. In our un-Christian selfishness we think that it is enough if we live an honorable personal life. We have too little that is contagious in our character. You see, not only evil, but also that which is good should be contagious, attractive and winning, spreading around like fire.

The history of the enthronement proves that it promotes this apostolic spirit. The greatest enemies of the Church, leaders of Freemasonry, converted in great numbers. It has been documented: "Very often the solemn enthronement in a family, among whose members one was spiritually dead or had left an empty place by becoming a prodigal, resulted in the return of the prodigal to the family whose consecration worked his great miracle." There we have it! The fire spreads. It becomes an apostolate.

We see that the enthronement of the most Sacred Heart of Jesus in the family is a providential work, in order to save mankind from the downfall threatening it. When Fr. Mateo wanted to come to France, it was suggested to him that he ought to wait until after the war. He answered with a question, which he directed to a bishop: "Did Noah build the ark after the deluge?" The deluge is there already. The ark is the Heart of Jesus. Let us go like Noah into the ark with the whole family. In that we save the family, let us make the family itself into an ark in which the highest goods of mankind are saved from the catastrophe which has already begun to overwhelm us.

We have never contested the importance of all the modern means of lifesaving, the importance of the Catholic press, Catholic organizations or Catholic politics. Despite all these aids we must never forget that the main task lies in the reconstruction of family life. The coming age must be the age of the family. There may well be lifeboats, but the ark in the deluge is the family filled with Catholic, supernatural spirit; the family whose King and Government is Christ. Here the sovereignty of God over state and society must be proclaimed and prepared.

THE KING OF THE SCHOOL

The parable of the sower is not only a parable of the priest, but also of the teacher. Every teacher is a sower who goes out to sow seed, whether he takes his seeds from the granary of the Lord or the powder magazine of hell. According to which he does, the teacher's vocation is either the most godly or the most devilish profession a person can take up. The teacher who acts not as a sower of truth, but rather of lies, is a devil!

If there were only enough millstones in the world, one ought to follow the advice of the Gospel and hang them around the necks of these seducers, so that they would sink into the depths of the sea. A bad sower, whether he be a teacher or a priest or a writer, is a national disaster, a poisoner of the wells of the public good. A nation that still hires such people and pays them out of public funds to instruct its youth has lost the last vestige of common sense, no matter how much democratic wisdom it may claim to have.

The example of every sower, whether priest, educator or writer, is Christ the Teacher, the Way, the Truth and the Life. For everyone who addresses himself to the people and especially the youth, Jesus' words in St. John (10:1-2) apply: "He that entereth not by the door into the sheepfold, but climbeth up another way, the same is a thief and a robber. But he that entereth in by the door is the shepherd of the sheep." The door of the school is, like the door of the Catholic Church, Jesus, Jesus the teacher!

The modern school has thrown Jesus out. It did not want Him to reign over it. The removal of the crucifixes from the classroom walls is only the outer sign of this anti-Christian education. The beginning of all political wisdom will lie in the triumphant carrying of the crucifix back into the teachers' colleges and into the schools by the nations. Jesus must again become the Teacher of the teachers, the King of the School! Without Him you can do nothing! All other teachers have the right to call themselves teachers only insofar as they have been pupils of this Teacher.

Jesus is the only Teacher of mankind, and therefore of the youth, in the full sense of the word. Others might claim this title in this or that subject and to this or that extent, but there is only one Teacher without any limitations. This Teacher knows everything. He is the Light of the world, which lights all who come into this world. Christ knows God. "Neither doth any one know the Father, but the Son, and he to whom it shall please the Son to reveal him" (Mt. 11:27).

Jesus knows the world. The world was made through Him and without Him was nothing made that was made. Jesus knows people, the human being as he ought to be and the human being as he is, man as he went forth from the hand of the Creator with his natural and supernatural capabilities and strengths, and fallen man with his evil inclinations.

Jesus is the greatest theologian and the greatest psychologist, and He is therefore the greatest teacher, the best expert on God and man, and therefore the best educator! There can be therefore no essential progress over and beyond Jesus in the science of education. Jesus, the Eternal Wisdom, created nothing halfway. The Gospel is sufficient for all places and all times, because it is the school of perfection.

Jesus is the teacher of the human race, not only because He says what the person ought to do and be, but also because He sets the example. We are taught not so much by that which we hear as through that which we see. According to an old proverb: Words move you, examples enthrall you.

The first rule which a teacher must keep in mind is that he himself does what he demands of others. No one can make others faithful, pious, obedient, humble or compassionate, if he is not so himself.

Great educators must always become, first of all, great persons themselves. The best teachers naturally must be the saints, whose lives call out to everyone: Follow the example! But the unreachable ideal of the educators of all times remains He Whom no one could blame of a sin, Jesus, the Most Holy. If others have something of the teacher *per se* in themselves, He has everything, because He teaches virtue through the divine classroom demonstration of His own life. A principal reason for our educational failures is that we have a lot of talkers and preachers, but few holy examples who studied education in the life of Jesus.

Jesus is the Teacher of mankind because He gives our souls not only truths, but also virtues. Truths alone are not sufficient, since education consists not only in enlightening the understanding, but also in strengthening the will, which has been weakened by original sin. That cannot come about through empty words, even the most magnificent calls to heroism, chivalry, self-government or human dignity. The storm of passion blows down such a house of cards.

It is a tenet of faith and a fact of experience that a complete education through purely natural means is impossible. The determining factor in the work of education is the Holy Spirit, or, what amounts to the same thing, the supernatural dynamics of grace which are transmitted through sacrifice, prayer and the Sacrament. Whoever wants to teach without sacrifice, prayer and the Sacrament, remains an unfruitful, though perhaps well-meaning chatterer. The doctrine of grace is the soul of educational theory. Whoever does not know this is no educator, even if he is a Catholic teacher.

Jesus is the Teacher of humanity, because no one ever underscored the necessity of teaching as He did. He came in order to create the new, supernatural man restored to the image and likeness of God, who is to become the inheritor of heaven. Everything—His life, His preaching, His suffering and death, the foundation of the Church—serves the requirements of this pedagogical goal of His work of redemption. Everything in Jesus is pedagogical. However, that which has no connection with the one thing necessary meets with no particular interest on the part of Jesus in His public ministry.

Despite the fact that He is omniscient and all laws of nature lie open before His eyes, He said not a word about them. Not a single discovery of natural science or any invention had anything to do with the public ministry of the Redeemer. Technology and industry received not the tiniest whisper of encouragement from Him. Although He is Infinite Beauty itself, He created no work of art, neither a statue nor a painting, neither a poem nor a musical piece. Although He is Eternal Love, he did nothing directly for so-called social reform, for medicine or for public health. Although He is the Friend of children, He did nothing, as far as we know, for primary and secondary education.

Why? Because all these things do not belong to that which is necessary. Jesus came to teach that which must be: faith, hope, love, patience, chastity, truthfulness, righteousness. The best teacher is the one who sets that which is necessary in the foreground and leaves unimportant and superfluous things in the background. Nowadays they do it the other way around.

Jesus is the Teacher of mankind, because in comparison to Him all teachers are only pupils. "But be not you called Rabbi (teacher). For one is your master; and all you are brethren....Neither be ye called masters; for one is your master, Christ" (Mt. 23:8,10). So it is written and so it is. Even today! Modern school wisdom does not want anymore to sit at the feet of Jesus. If it quotes, it does not quote a word of God, but rather human words like those of Rousseau, Pestalozzi or whoever else counts as "great" among little people.

We do not deny that people can write true and good things in educational science. But the true and the good, that which is really true and good in the fullest sense of the word, was already said by Him who nearly two thousand years ago went out to sow seed. All that the scholars can do is to formulate Jesus' teaching anew, apply it, collect it. We have to expect no other in the science of education. The Messiah of the school has already come. We have nothing to do other than to hear and to proclaim Him. The seed is the Word of God.

Today the world is seething with questions and problems. Yet the question of questions is this: Do you want to bring Christ, Who has been banned from the school by the spirit of unbelief in a materialistic time and by your cowardliness, back into the school? Ought Christ the Teacher to become once again the educator and teacher of your children? This is not just a question of the crucifix in the classroom; it is a matter of the personality, the spirit, the word and the grace of Christ, His reign over the souls and hearts, His kingdom. Whatever else we do will prove useless if we forget this one necessary thing. Not the social battle over bread and money shall change the face of the earth, but rather the fight for Christ's school. If the divine Sower does not go out to sow, then all else is useless.

THE KING OF KINGS

Some modern states still have their national day of prayer. It is the last twilight of a disappearing age. Afterward, I fear, comes the night, the black night with harsh lightning flashes and loud thunder and trembling earth and pale people—the night when people no longer pray, the night of sin and revenge, the night of the deluge.

And then, I hope, will come the new day. On that day no one will need prayer days anymore, because people will pray at all times and in all places. Instead of the day of prayer will come the year of prayer. Remember that you keep holy the day of prayer, the last and only day on which the modern state turns to the people and says, *orate fratres*—pray, brethren...

The times are not favorable to days of prayer. This island will also sink, and no one will save it. The national day of prayer will fall, because it stands in opposition to the modern concept of the state. The modern political heresy is the state without religion, the laicized state. The official relations between state and Church will be severed. Perhaps the two will have a rendezvous once a year. By judicial pronouncement of people and government, the two have received a legal separation. They say it's better so: for hundreds of years he is supposed to have mistreated her so much that separation is a relief for her. Maybe! The separation of the Church from the modern state may well be in the interests of the Church in some countries.

But I am opposed to the error which is even widespread in Catholic circles, which says that separation is divorce, as though certain connections between Church and state, which exist on the basis of unchangeable natural laws, could ever be torn asunder. I understand the "day of prayer" for this reason. It says to me:

State without Church is social deicide! I know no other word for it. Whoever divorces the body from the soul commits murder. And murder is a crime. State and Church belong together like body and soul. The state is the body. The physical, earthly well-being of the people is its purpose. The Church is the soul. The spiritual, supernatural happiness of the people is her goal. The soul must therefore remain in the body. The Church must be active in the state. To separate them is murder. And that is exactly what they want. Religion ought not to be the soul of the state anymore. God has nothing more to do with the temporal affairs of the nation.

I can understand this sentence if I hear it out of the mouth of an unbeliever. For if God is non-existent, then this nonentity of course has nothing to do with anything. Likewise I understand this declaration if it comes from the pen of a deist, according to whose world view God was sent into retirement after the creation of the world and the world is completely left to its own devices. But I shall never be able to understand how one can pray the first sentence of the Creed, can believe in an Almighty, Omniscient, Omnipresent God, and at the same time exclude Him from the government of temporal affairs.

If God is God, then He is eternal, everywhere and in everything. If man is a creature, then he is always, everywhere and in everything God's creature. If Question One of my catechism is correct, I am on earth in order to serve God, and I am that always, everywhere and in everything. Every single action of mine must be in accordance with the will of God and with my goal and end. That is a rule without any exceptions! No dispensations!

This is also the highest law of the statesman, the politician, the judge, the official, the citizen, valid for every legislation, every judgment, every public work, every election and every vote. The soul of public life in its entirety is the remembrance of God, of our goal in life and vocation, the norm of our life, in short: religion.

It may be possible to cut off official communication between Church and state, but you can never legally separate the citizen and the statesman from his Lord God, from his conscience, from his Ten Commandments, his religious convictions, in other words his Church. He will always have basic principles according to which he acts. And if these principles are not Catholic, then they are Protestant, freethinking, materialistic or socialist; they are thus the principles of a particular religion or world view, but they are never neutral.

As his God is, so will be his policy! As his God is, so will be his law books! As his God is, so will be his schools! As his God is, so will be his courts of law! There may be an official separation between Church and state, but there is no divorce. The spirit of the Church must remain the soul of the state. What God has joined together, cannot be separated by man. To separate God's truth from the laws of public life is social deicide. And social deicide is social suicide.

The state without the Church is the death of the state. The body without the soul is a corpse! To the degree in which the influence of the Church on public life disappears, we observe two signs of approaching death: dying authority and dying freedom. The state can only exist by reason of its authority. It rests upon the precondition that there are governments that are recognized, laws that are obeyed, orders that are carried out, judgments that are accepted as valid. Therein lies the guarantee of order, peace, well-being and safety.

However, the protector of the authority of the state is the Church.

It is a holy principle of faith for the Church that everyone bow to the power of the state. Whoever "resisteth the power, resisteth the ordinance of God. And they that resist purchase to themselves damnation" (Rom. 13:2). According to the teaching of St. Paul, the authority of the state is thus a part of that Gospel of which no single word shall die. The Church is the foundation of the state.

However, as soon as the government is no longer regarded as God's servant and as a power appointed by Him, it leaves itself hanging in the air. Why should anyone obey? What is a worker? A human being! What is a cabinet member? No more than the worker: a human being! Why should one man command and the other obey him? Why should one obey the laws? Who makes them? People, human beings just like I am. And with what right do ten thousand or thirty thousand voters, who vote "yes" on a referendum, say to me "Thou shalt!" if I decide to say: "I won't!"

Authority, *i.e.,* a person above me, only exists if One Who is really higher sets him over me, and that can only be if God, religion and the Church exist. If religion does not stand with the fiery sword of the Cherubim next to the state, then the latter is nothing but presumptuousness, and as a logical consequence there exists the right of disobedience, of revolution and of anarchy.

Secondly, the state exists only as a humanly worthy institution insofar as it guarantees not only the authority of the government, but also the freedom of the people. That country is the happiest which has the most rights and freedoms and the least laws and commands. There exists a law of world history: The more religion, the more freedom.

Therefore: the less religion, the more force. "The religious temperature of a country cannot rise, without the temperature of political force falling in inverse proportion; and on the other hand, the religious temperature of a country cannot fall without at the same time the temperature of political force rising even to the point of tyranny." (*Cf.* Juan Donoso Cortés, *Address on Dictatorship before the Spanish Parliament*, Jan. 4, 1849.)

Before the day of Golgotha, the temperature of religion had sunk to zero, while the fever of the omnipotent state had reached 110^0. There were only tyrants and slaves. Then Jesus appeared. The religious thermometer reached its highest peak and with it the level of freedom. Jesus together with His disciples formed a society, and in this society there was no force. Among Jesus and His disciples there was no other government than that of love, the love of the Master for His followers. Contrast this with the French Revolution: religion is down to 0^0 and freedom is also at 0^0. Under the shadow of the guillotine, violence rose to fever pitch, and from July 1, 1789, to October 26, 1795, a total of 15,479 laws were passed.

Only one force protects the citizen from the deformation of state power into freedom-killing tyranny: the "thou shalt" and the "thou shalt not" of religion, spoken to the princely thrones and the green seat cushions of the congresses. The state without the Church is social suicide, the death of authority above and the death of freedom below!

National day of prayer, you are a lighthouse in the fog! Day of my God! Day of my people! Your meaning is state and God, Church and people, these two equal one! What God hath joined together, let not man put asunder (Mk. 10:9)!

THE KING ON THE CROSS

Following the destruction of Jerusalem, the Romans covered the places of hallowed memory to the Christian with rubble. The cave of the Holy Sepulchre was buried under such rubble, and over it as well as over Golgotha pagan images and temples were erected in honor of Venus and Jupiter. For this reason the Christians did not go there anymore, in order not to be mistaken for idol-worshippers. Emperor Constantine ordered the temples and images torn down and the rubble carried away. After long and hard work the cave of the Holy Sepulchre was found. Not far away three crosses with nails were discovered, and along with them the superscription, which, however, lay separate from the cross.

Without doubt one of these must be the Cross of the Savior, but there was no certain sign that would differentiate it from the crosses of the two thieves. This was given when a mortally ill woman was suddenly cured by touching the true Cross. The Holy Cross was then encased in silver and precious gems, and a church was built over it, which according to Emperor Constantine's order was to be more magnificent than anything ever seen before. In memory of these events, the Church recalls the Finding of the Most Holy Cross on May 3, in order that on every day until the Feast of the Exaltation of the Cross (September 14), land and people will be blessed with a splinter, a particle of the Cross.

We have every reason to remember these events. Christianity is the religion of the Crucified One. In his first letter to the Corinthians the Apostle of the Nations, St. Paul, declares: "For I judged not myself to know anything among you, but Jesus Christ, and him crucified" (I Cor. 2:2). St. Paul's preaching, no matter how many-sided it appears, always returns to the central Sun of Christendom: Jesus on the Cross, King of the World! Everything else is either a ray from this Sun, or it is nothing. In the Crucifix lies our entire dogmatic and moral theology, our entire teaching on faith and morals, our catechism. The Cross is our library. Every other book has value only inasmuch as the spirit of the Cross speaks in it.

Modernists have attempted to ban the old preaching of St. Paul, the Gospel of the Cross, to oblivion. The Cross means the teaching of the necessity of sacrifice and of grace, and this now lies under the rubble on which a new paganism has erected once again the pagan images and temples of Jupiter and Mercury, Venus and Bacchus—in other words, the absolutist state, capitalism, immorality and addiction to pleasure. A certain superficial Christianity, which puts more value on being modern than on being Catholic and Biblical, and for which the imitation of the spirit of the times is more understandable than the imitation of Christ, has made itself a willing accomplice.

We have lost the Cross. We have a Christianity that no longer understands sacrifice and therefore is no Christianity or only a soulless version of Christianity. We need Constantines and Helens who will once again dig out the Cross from under the rubble and make it their shrine and their sign, and who believe that the King's throne is the Cross.

The crucified King! In the family we must have a Finding of the Most Holy Cross! The modern family has lost the crucifix, and in its place it has raised up the political hero, the artist, old pagan gods, nudity and the prostitute. The crucifix does not fit into the modern home. The modern living room preaches money-grabbing, pride, vanity, lasciviousness, laziness. The modern living room is the exaltation of the seven deadly sins. At least one is honest enough to feel that the Cross no longer fits into this milieu and has got rid of it. People have gotten rid of it because in the long run the crucifix can only remain there where the spirit of the Crucified One remains, and the spirit of the Crucified is no longer there.

The spirit of the Crucified is the spirit of love and sacrifice, but the spirit of the modern family is the spirit of selfishness and enjoyment. The speech of the Crucified says: First the others, I come last! The speech of selfishness is: First I, then again I, the others come last! The Christian family is built on the notion of sacrifice and devotion. The concept of the Christian father is: Work from morning to evening for others. The concept of the Christian mother is: Care for others! Let the self always come last! The concept of the Christian child is: Respect, love, obedience. Father and Mother first, only then I!

This notion of sacrifice and devotion is dying out in the modern family. The modern family is built upon the law of egotism. The modern family takes as its motto: "As much enjoyment and as little sacrifice as possible!" That is the source of Malthusianism. That is where characterless education comes from. And that is the doom of this family. Only the Cross and its sermon of self-discipline, self-denial and devotion can save the dying family.

The crucified King! The Finding of the Cross must also take place in the shop. It used to be that just as in all phases of life, the workshop was lit by the light of religion. It was a sort of shrine. Work was considered service to God and to the neighbor. It was not mere breadwinning and money-making. Since it was a place of service to God, the workroom was dominated by the crucifix. The crucifix was the highest standard of work for the artisan, a constant spurring on to diligence, conscientiousness, truthfulness, honesty, patience, gentleness, perseverance. In the shadow of the crucifix, greed, stinginess, shady business practices, fraud, overpricing, unjust wages, degrading treatment of workers, envy and class hatred could not occur or at least never attained the status of a general social disease. Liberalism has banned the Cross from the workshop by proclaiming the heresy that religion and work, morals and industry or commerce have nothing to do with one another. It believes it can replace the crucifix with policing, regulations and legal paragraphs.

Experience has proven the impossibility of this economic theory, which has made the workshop, the studio, the office and the factory into a battleground of wild passion, where one class becomes wolf and snake for the other. The place of work must again dig out the lost Cross from under the rubble of capitalism and socialism. The worker together with the boss must carry the crucifix in triumph back to its old place of honor. Otherwise both are lost, irreversibly lost. The social question will either be resolved by the Cross, that is, by the spirit of sacrifice, of brotherly love, or it will not be resolved at all.

The crucified King! The Feast of the Finding of the Cross must also be the feast of the school. The school, from elementary school to university, was founded by the Catholic Church. The Church is the supernatural educator of the peoples, as the family is the natural teacher of the nations. The divine and the natural law hand over the child to its father, its mother and the priest for its education. Whoever instructs and raises the child beyond father, mother and priest only does so on contract to these three persons. The state is not a teacher. The state is official, lawgiver, judge, policeman and soldier, but it is not a teacher. The state compulsory school is a robbery perpetrated against the family, the Church and the child.

We demand the free Catholic school. We demand that the school be given back to its rightful owners, the family and the Church. We demand as the only help, without which all politics, all church building and all organizing are of no use: the repetition of the work of Constantine and St. Helen, the excavation of the Cross lost by liberal school policy. The Finding of the Cross and the Exaltation of the Cross are the soul of our school policy. And school policy is the soul of every other policy!

The crucified King! The Finding of the Cross, the program of family, economic and educational reform, is finally also the goal of political reform. Pope St. Pius X once said: "Our policy is the Cross!" That says a great deal. The Cross is obedience, even under the most difficult conditions; it is respect for the governments instituted by God. Our policy is recognition of every lawful authority. The Cross is patience, when one cannot achieve everything good and right at once. Our policy is sacrifice. The Cross is solidarity, devotion to all. Our policy is the solidarity of persons, classes, states of life, nations and people.

The Cross is fidelity even unto martyrdom. It is preferring to die rather than to dishonor oneself with cowardliness, betrayal and false compromises. Our policy is the Catholic fidelity promised in Baptism and Confirmation. The Cross is giving up immediate success in confidence in the unfailing, final triumph of the cause of God. Our policy is trust in God. The Cross is the will rather to remain alone, when our conscience demands it, than to run with the majority or the party. Our policy is courage to be unpopular. The Cross is the source of grace. Our policy is belief in the supernatural, in grace, prayer, the sacraments, Mary, St. Michael. The international policy of all parties has lost the Cross. That is the cause of the general collapse of all so-called law-and-order parties. Until politics has again found the Cross, all efforts will be in vain. The Crucified One must become King!

THE KING'S ENTHRONEMENT

Bartholomaeus Holzhauser, who died in the year 1658 in the town of Bingen on the Rhine, predicted our times as the period in which the princedoms and monarchies would be overthrown. All the peoples would conspire to erect free states. This time has come. One king after another has been forced to step down from his throne. And in this time, in which the sinister ghost of the revolution wanders about in the world and knocks on the doors of the palaces of princes and kings, the Catholic world chose to proclaim a spiritual kingship in all countries. The King is not an unknown. For nearly two thousand years no name is more often mentioned in all the languages of the world. Before Him every knee must bow, in heaven, on earth and below the earth.

The concept of Jesus' kingship already accompanied the annunciation of His birth: "...and the Lord God shall give unto him the throne of David his father....And of his kingdom there shall be no end" (Lk. 1:32-33). These words belong to the angel's message. Christ will be a King! But for quite some time there was confusion among Jesus' disciples as to the nature of this kingship. Many dreamed of a political Messiah with military might and earthly wealth. Christ destroyed this madness with all decisiveness. When after the miraculous multiplication of the loaves five thousand men wanted to raise Him to the throne, He fled from them.

As decisive as this rejection of political enthronement is, just as definite is the affirmation of the spiritual and religious enthronement in the most critical hour of Our Lord. As a condemned man, betrayed and abandoned, He declares at the very moment when the misled people reject His kinghip in a public vote: My kingdom is not of this world. But I am a King. For this I have come into the world. Then they led Him out to Golgotha and nailed Him to a cross. They did not know what they were doing. Yet in obedience to a higher will, Pilate wrote the inscription upon the cross: Jesus of Nazareth, the King! That was the first solemn, public enthronement of the Sacred Heart of Jesus.

The bloody enthronement was followed by the others. In three hundred years, paganism was overcome in the Roman world empire. When Emperor Constantine proclaimed the freedom of the

Christian religion in 313, what else was it but a solemn, public enthronement of Christ the King on the part of the state? Christ is King, King of Minds, King of Hearts, King of public life. You know what has happened. For the last four to five hundred years, a new, modern spirit has been working to bring Christ down from His throne. A dark Good Friday broke over the Church. The cry of the first Good Friday became the slogan of the new one.

"We do not want Him to reign over us!" cried the statesmen, the politicians, the princes, the governments, the representatives and the voters. "Religion has nothing to do with politics." The spiritual kingship of Christ in national life was overthrown. "We do not want Him to reign over us!" cried the intellectuals, the writers, the professors, the teachers. "Religion has nothing to do with science and the schools." The kingdom of Jesus in the world of thought, in the school, in literature and in the press was overthrown. "We do not want Him to reign over us!" cried the bankers, the businessmen, the factory managers, the artisans, the union secretaries and the workers. "Religion has nothing to do with economic life, with commerce, industry and trade." The spiritual kingdom of Jesus over the world of work and business was overthrown.

"We do not want Him to reign over us!" cried the men and women, the sons and daughters. "Religion has nothing to do with marriage and the family." The spiritual kingship of Jesus over homelife was overthrown.

What remained for Christ? The tabernacle, the sacristy, the Church. If the expulsion of Christ from this, His last holy domain, were to succeed, then His reign on earth would be abolished.

But tabernacles have remained for the Redeemer. And it will be from the tabernacle outward that Christ will reconquer the spiritual kingship over the world. First in the families, then in the schools, then in the sciences, in politics, in society, in the working world. That is the sense of the Enthronement. Just as the Jews, after they had eaten the miraculous bread, wanted to make Jesus into a political king, so also we want, ever since we and our little ones learned in the days of the great pope of the Eucharist, St. Pius X, to partake often of the miraculous Bread of Heaven, the Communion, to make Christ our spiritual King out of gratitude. Enthronement of the Sacred Heart of Jesus!

A new time has come. The peoples have wanted new laws, new governments; there have been overthrows and abdications everywhere. What do we want? What all the world is doing, that we can do also: not just a bit of mending work, no, revolution! Change! A new government! But truly Catholic revolutions are not like liberal, socialist and anarchist revolutions. We need no swords, no guns, no dynamite and no barricades for our revolutions. We need no force. We shed not one drop of blood.

The Catholic change is the opposite of revolution. We overthrow hatred in order to replace it with love, injustice in order to replace it with justice, lies in order to replace them with truth, disorder in order to replace it with order. Freemasonry and socialism want to erect a world republic by means of revolutions and wars. We want to erect not a political, but rather a spiritual world monarchy. We want to raise to its throne the only One Who has a right to be King of all minds and hearts, first because He is God, secondly because He is the Savior, thirdly because He alone can bring happiness to the individual and to the peoples. We want the Enthronement of the Sacred Heart of Jesus.

Because no one can erect a new government except upon the ruins of the old, we want the overthrow of the reign of the devil, the overthrow of unbelief, of hatred, of injustice, of the immorality which poisons everything. Because every building must begin with the foundation, we want to begin with the families. We want new governments in the family homes, before we can establish new governments in the schoolhouses, in city hall and in the factories. We want it.

Let us act today as though we were in a parliament. We are here in order to solemnly recognize the kingdom of Jesus. We are as serious about it as we ever were about anything in our lives. Kneel down! There is your King, up front. There is His picture, witness forever to this holy hour. Answer: Do you want the King of the tabernacle to be King of your minds and hearts? And the solemn cry goes up: Yes, we want it!

Do you want the Divine Heart of Jesus to reign above all in your families? Yes, we want it! Children, boys, girls, men, women, do you want to work through prayer and word and good example for the goal that Jesus be ever more known, loved, and glorified in your parish? Yes, we want it! Do you want this picture to be no mere decoration and this ceremony no empty ritual, but rather a program, a milestone in the history of the parish? Yes, we want it! Do you want this day of the Enthronement of the Sacred Heart of Jesus to be a holy and honored day for all the future? Yes, we want it!

It is enough. The act will be recorded in the protocols of heaven: Our parish will in the future be a parish of the Sacred Heart of Jesus, Christ our King!

THE KING'S REALM

Once the representatives of the Freethinking Imperialist Party—as we might call the Herodians—and the Conservative Nationalists, *i.e.,* the Pharisees, directed a so-called political interpellation to Jesus: they questioned Christ about the question of imperial taxes. The Savior gave short, concise replies, so that the delegation was astonished. They had found One Who knew more than they. They soon had enough, left Him and went away.

Once again theology triumphed over politics. It was as much later the anarchist Proudhon had to admit: It is amazing how we always find theology, *i.e.,* the science of God, at the deepest base of our politics. But Jesus began to preach. From the emperor He went on to God. Today we ought to do just the same.

In our times a deep longing goes through many parts of the world, a desire for a strong personality who would bring law and order, a dictator who would close the parliaments, or a great monarch. One alone must reign! This one person whom the peoples await will have to be either a great tyrant, an Antichrist, a man of sin and demonic evil, or it will be a Prince of Peace, a father of the peoples, a man of unflinching justice, a savior, a holy emperor.[2]

Whether the one or the other stands outside the gate, God alone knows. But whether the future brings us the one or the other, in the last analysis it will again be a question of theology: whether one comes who will give God everything that is God's, or one who takes everything away from God; either one who will dedicate him-

---

[2] It must be borne in mind that Fr. Mäder wrote this prophetic article in the 1920's! (Translator's note)

self completely to the service of the world empire of Jesus, the Son of God, or conversely to the service of a world empire of Satan, the Antichrist.

When we talk of emperors, we declare today that our Emperor, our great Monarch is Jesus. Jesus is Emperor in the realm of space: He has the most extensive of all monarchies. His kingdom is all-present. It extends over the entire world, and this on the basis of incontestable, inalienable titles. He is the great Monarch, not by the will of His subjects, but by the power of His nature. He is King of the World, because He is its Owner; he is Owner because He is its Creator. In contrast to other princes, He has created His realm Himself, down to the last particle of dust and the last atom. Every being therein exists because He willed that it be, and only because He willed that it be! All things were made by Him, says St. John (Jn. 1:3).

Jesus is King in the realm of heaven. "And I beheld, and I heard the voice of many angels round about the throne,...saying with a loud voice: The Lamb that was slain is worthy to receive power, and divinity, and wisdom, and strength, and honor, and benediction" (Apoc. 5:11-12). Jesus is the great Monarch of heaven!

Jesus is King of the earth, "the prince of the kings of the earth" (Apoc. 1:5). The Lord of lords! The nations are given "for thy inheritance, and the uttermost parts of the earth for thy possession" (Ps. 2:8). He rules them with a rod of iron and, if He will, breaks them in pieces like a potter's vessel (*Ibid.*). Jesus is the great Monarch on earth! We have to emphasize this most strongly. Modern Liberalism may be perhaps so generous as to recognize a certain kingship over heaven for Him, or at least to tolerate it, but it does not want to hear anything of a spiritual, universal monarchy of Christendom on earth and of the exclusive, world-wide reign of Christianity among mankind.

According to the liberal view, the earth ought to remain a free colony, in which the settlement policy of Satan cannot be hindered by any reactionary limitations according to law and constitution. That is the sense of the gigantic cultural battle of our time: whether the King of heaven should also be King of the earth, politics, economy, art and science not excluded; or whether the Lord of heaven is only allowed to be tolerated by the Freemasons and liberals as a foreigner on the earth He created.

We shall go yet further. If we announce the universal kingship of Jesus in the entire realm of space, then we cannot even exclude hell from this. As the Apocalypse states, Christ has "the keys of death and of hell" (Apoc. 1:18). Even those under the earth must bend their knees before Him. He is also King in the realm of justice. Satan is not some kind of co-god. He is only God's jailor. Christ alone is King!

We have preached the kingship of Jesus in the realm of space. We also preach the kingship of Jesus in the realm of time. This means: As it was in the beginning, is now and ever shall be. His kingdom shall have no end. He is the immortal King of the centuries. St. Teresa of Avila became ecstatic with joy whenever she heard the words of the Nicene Creed: "His kingdom shall have no end."

Jesus is the immortal King in a double sense. In the first place, He reigns without interruption. Human governments do not always reign, whether because they have not the time or the good will or the understanding to do so. There are sleeping, lame, blind, deaf and dumb governments which are alive in name, but in fact are dead. The government of Jesus is just the opposite: it is all-present, all-powerful, all-knowing, all-wise. It reigns all the time, orders and guides all things, the smallest as well as the largest. Nothing escapes its gaze, its arms, its heart, by day or by night.

Thus the government of Jesus Christ reigns without ceasing. It has no ministerial or departmental crises, no firings and no abdications, no revolutions. In the Department of External Affairs, that is in the visible government of the Church and on the level of the bishops, there can arise serious crises. Individual shepherds can fail in their office, and in individual regions the Church organization can even die out completely. But the actual, invisible government, the reign of Christ over the souls, remains, whether we notice it or not.

We do not know what the future will bring. It can bring the same as the past brought. Imagine just as an example the worst case: a collapsing St. Peter's, a burning Vatican, a pope abandoned and fleeing, fallen away priests and bishops, a general persecution of the Church, the dwellers on earth drunk, as the Apocalypse says, with "the wine of the great harlot, who sitteth upon many waters" (Apoc. 17:1), with the wine of international Freemasonry, the world drunk with "the blood of the saints" and the witnesses of Jesus Christ (*Cf.* Apoc. 17:6). The whole earth a field of ruins!

The Apocalypse predicts similar and even more frightful things for the age of the great beast, the Antichrist. But even in these fearsome times of catastrophe, the King of Eternity does not sleep. This same Apocalypse that draws such grim pictures suddenly changes the scene: "And I heard as it were the voice of a great multitude, and as the voice of many waters, and as the voice of great thunders, saying, "Alleluia: for the Lord our God the Almighty hath reigned" (Apoc. 19:6).

"And I saw heaven opened, and behold a white horse; and he that sat upon him was called faithful and true, and with justice doth he judge and fight. And his eyes were as a flame of fire, and on his head were many diadems,...and his name is called, THE WORD OF GOD. And the armies that are in heaven followed him on white horses, clothed in fine linen, white and clean. And out of his mouth proceedeth a sharp, two-edged sword; that with it he may strike the nations. And he shall rule them with a rod of iron....And he hath on his garment...written: KING OF KINGS AND LORD OF LORDS" (Apoc. 19:11-16).

They want to force Him to abdicate, the modernists, the liberals, the non-denominationalists, the Freemasons. Yet He is and remains King, King of heaven and of earth, immortal King of the centuries, Emperor in the empire of time.

"Render therefore to Caesar the things that are Caesar's, and to God the things that are God's" (Lk. 20:25). Interest and taxes are too little. Interest and taxes, parts of the whole sum, are paid to the mighty of this earth. But to your Emperor, the King of Love, you must give not just a part, but everything, above all the most precious thing: the realm of the heart, the kingdom of love. The portrait and the inscription on the coin decides over the duty of the citizen to pay taxes. The image of your soul belongs to God; the inscription is Jesus. Therefore render to God the things that are God's, all of them!

THE KING'S PARTY

The waters of the flood rise higher and higher. More and more threatening is the lightning in the clouds in which the fate of the peoples of Europe rests. Less and less soluble appears the world crisis for the calm observer. The ghost of deadly despair sneers: You are all lost!

The highest achievements of modern culture sink into the red sea of socialism; the almighty state, militarism, science, organization and capital fail. All the foundations of order tremble. All the governments have no solutions.

We have eaten of the forbidden fruit—in 1517 and in 1789! Now we are standing around freezing, hungry and naked, and are ashamed. Our eyes have been opened. We hear the voice of God in the terrible events of the last decades and in those threatening to happen in the future.

Even though the great mass today still knows nothing but the fleshpots of economic reforms and the dance around the golden calf, the more noble part of the people is beginning to grasp that salvation does not come from the bakers and the butchers alone. For the peoples do not live on bread alone, but rather from every word that comes from the mouth of God.

A new Europe must arise, and the new Europe that will come to be after the deluge in order, like the sower, to sow the seed of God's kingdom in the furrows ploughed by the terrible plow of disaster, should and must be a Catholic Europe. You will not be able to beat this new race to death, not with all the clubs of your parties, because it will be full of the Holy Spirit and ready to live and die for His cause.

It is Gospel truth that you must pour new wine into new wineskins. Parties will not suffice. The Holy Father has demanded Catholic Action over and above all parties. In many ways we think, speak and act other than do parties. We want to be ourselves, and we can only do that if we stand on our own feet on the soil of Catholic Action.

We shall bring down from heaven the stars on our banners. We distrust fashionable slogans. We are Catholic. Our Catholic party is therefore really no party. The Catholic party must be Catholic.

That which flames up in the heart should shine from the galaxies and burn in our hands to make them thirsty for deeds. All the world should know who we are. We are tired of playing dumb, of keeping still out of cautiousness, or of speaking differently from what we think and acting differently than we believe.

We want to be a party of God's followers. The great Pope St. Pius X demanded it: "The only kind of party of order that can really bring peace into our ruined relationships is the party of the followers of God. We must therefore advance it and increase the number of its members as much as possible, if we are moved by love of orderly conditions."

Our program is God, the program of St. Michael. We demand the rights of God to His world and fight therefore with all the popes of the last hundred and more years against the liberal, modern rights of man, which in reality are nothing more than the right of the false against the true, the bad against the good, revolution against order, sin against the Most High.

We are thus against everything that is against God. We declare war against law without God, marriage without God, science and school without God, the common good without God, work without God—in other words, laicism in all areas.

He Who created the world must again become its Lord, and His commandments on their two tablets the basis and norm of our legal codes! Let politics be service to God! The unhappy gulf between religion and public life must disappear. Let us serve one master instead of showing our lack of character by serving two! We cry out in all the alleyways: I believe in God, the Almighty, the Creator of heaven and earth! The One God lives!

We are a party of Christ the King. All policy that is ashamed of this Name should be cleaned out of the parliaments of Christian nations. Christ must reign in the legislative bodies! We were not baptized and confirmed for nothing. It should be obvious when we speak.

The world cries out of chaos for the coming Savior. The secret Emperor is the God of our tabernacles, Christ the Way, the Truth and the Life. He is the One Who should and will come. We must all bow the knee before Him. Long live Jesus! We campaign for Christ, the immortal King of the centuries. The twentieth century must become the century of Jesus, after the 19th has been named the century of Mary. We want to be the trailblazers, at home and outdoors, so that the Kingdom of Christ, the Enthronement of Our Lord become reality, European reality, worldwide reality, since it has become religious reality. For Christ is King! We are the party of the sons of Rome. We are Catholic. We expect all salvation from the true Church alone, from her who is called, now as so often in the course of history, to be the ark in the deluge. "There are only two powers in the world. The Catholic Church is the one superpower in the realm of the spirit, and the other superpower stands in opposition to her: the revolution. Everything in between is powerlessness."

Was not the decade after World War I a course in apologetics in which the world itself demonstrated the rightness of this sentence? The proofs became clearer every day. All the card houses fell down. All the crutches broke. All the artificial dikes against the overthrow were undermined. That the collapse of all order did not occur sooner must be seen as a miracle of the divine mercy.

Rome or Moscow, that is the question. Whoever does not openly stand on the side of the Church serves, consciously or unconsciously, the revolution. The leaders of the nations have nothing better and more necessary to do than to point to the dogma of the ninth Article of Faith at every opportunity ("the holy, catholic Church"). This can be done only by one movement, the Catholic one, which is not limited by alliances and compromises and for whom the salvation of mankind stands above small and fleeting successes.

This movement must become a fact. It is the most urgent national and international necessity. It is not enough for priests to talk about the pope from the pulpit. Even the statesmen must listen to the voice that goes out from the Vatican Hill, the Mt. Sinai of the New Covenant. Rome or Moscow!

You ask what are our tactics: the same as always. We campaign above all on our Catholic knees. We campaign like all the great politicians of the Old and the New Covenant. We shoot down the superstition that victory is essentially the result of big numbers and full bank accounts. In the life of the nations as in the lives of individuals, everything depends upon the First Politician, God. We are not embarrassed to put that into our party platform. It would be nonsense to want to fight and win for God but without Him.

God wills it! Now it should blow like the storm of Pentecost through all the valleys and glow on all the heights like a holy signal fire. God wills it! We know that our way is marked with the sign of Golgotha. Our policy is the Cross! Never were great things accomplished in any other way. That is why we happily lay goods and blood on the high altar of our King. We want to be a people of heroes, not one of scared rabbits, and to be ready to risk everything for the Highest.

Now blow the trumpet of the dawn, beat the drums to assemble the troops! Catholic people, wake up! Your honor, your salvation and your conscience are at risk. It is a question of the Greatest and the Last. Let the name "Catholic" be your slogan! In the name of the Lord of Hosts! Forward march!

RUNNING AWAY FROM THE KING

All festivals of Our Lord are Catholic feasts, but perhaps it is allowed to call the Feast of Christ the King the most Catholic of all feastdays. As Pope Pius XI wrote in his encyclical *Quas Primas*, the mysteries of the life of Jesus Christ celebrated in the course of the year receive their crowning through the Feast of Christ as King. The Kingship of Christ is as central as a sun for the whole of Christianity. One cannot say more, but one may also not say less. That is why the attitude toward the absolute and universal idea of Christ the King is in a certain sense the mark of the Catholicity of a people and a time. The mark of the present liberal period of the world is the flight from Christ's kingship. The mark of the future must be that it is a definitely anti-liberal Age of Christ the King.

The modern world has travelled in stages, so to speak, on the route of its flight from the kingship of Jesus to its deadly leap into the abyss. Social godlessness was not developed in one day's time. The poison of godlessness hidden in the veins of the states has its anamnesis, the history of its illness. The encyclical on Christ the King differentiates four stages in the development of the illness. The first stage is deism. "One begins by denying the kingship of Christ over all peoples." Out of this masonic deism stems the second stage, that of political naturalism: "One denies the right of the Church, which itself derives from the right of Jesus Christ, to teach the human race, to make laws, to guide the peoples, in order to lead them to everlasting happiness."

The third stage grows out of political naturalism: Liberalism. "Step by step the Christian religion was placed unworthily on the same level with other, false religions." The fourth stage, prepared by Liberalism, is the tyrannical omnipotence of the state. "Religion was subjected to worldly power and abandoned to the arbitrary will of princes and governments."

The first stage in the flight of the modern world from Jesus the King is the denial of Christ's rule over the peoples. Thus one begins with a sin of the intelligence. Like every revolution, the great anti-Christian revolution of the modern period begins at the top, in the head, with a false idea, an erroneous teaching. The error is called deism. Deism says: "There is a God. There is a Supreme being. There is a Builder of the Universe. That is clear. Atheism is nonsense. But after he built the world, the Great Builder retired and left the world to its fate."

The god of deism does not reign. The god of deism has no power. The god of deism is not king. Above all he is not the unlimited, all-embracing, sole Ruler of the universe. He is not King of kings, Lord of lords, Lawgiver of lawgivers, Judge of judges! Deism takes away from God His crown and scepter. It commits the greatest robbery of world history. Adam stole an apple. Deism steals from God the orb of the world. The god of deism is blind, deaf, dumb and lame. He is a god of powerlessness. That is the Fall out of which all liberal evil and unhappiness has come over the modern world. That is the first stage of the flight of modern man from Christ the King: deism's false concept of God!

The second stage of society's flight from Christ the King is political naturalism. After unbelieving science has prepared the poison of heresy in its laboratory, it will now inject it into the veins of the state. First it is injected into the brain, that is the government. The god of deism does not bother about the state. It is therefore logical that for its part politics does not bother about God. Constitutions and laws are made without paying attention to the laws of Sinai and the Gospels. One acts as though there were no Christ and no

Church. An individual senator may go to Mass; Congress does not. An individual civil servant may be religious as a private citizen, but the bureaucracy is non-denominational.

We have run so far away from Christ the King that one may speak of social atheism and social deicide. The state acts as though there were no God and as though the state were the omniscient, omnipresent, almighty God. The modern state as such is godless. The state acts as though Jesus Christ were not the Redeemer, the Teacher, the Lord and Judge of mankind. It repeats the crime of Golgotha. The modern state as such is anti-Christian. The state acts as though the Catholic Church were not the pillar and foundation of truth, the mother and teacher of the nations. The modern state as such is an enemy of the Church. The flight from the kingdom of Christ has already become the greatest official fact of modern society.

Now comes the third stage in the flight from Christ the King: Liberalism. The poison seeps down from the head into the members, from the constitution into the customs, from the government into the people. If the state needs no religion, then it is clear that the citizen must be free to take on and practice atheism. Truth and error, Church and sect, Christ and Barabbas, the unbeliever and the believer have equal rights. Error, unbelief and complete godlessness are declared on the basis of the constitutions to be holy and inalienable human rights. Once freedom is loosed from responsibility to the Most High, it becomes revolutionary. Freedom of belief becomes freedom of non-belief; freedom of conscience becomes freedom of unscrupulousness; freedom of religion becomes freedom to have no religion. Running away from Christ the King, once a privilege of so-called intellectuals, has finally become the basic law of modern nations.

Today the overthrow of Christ the King in the public life of the peoples is a clear fact to all eyes. We cannot prevent Christ from ruling. Christ the King reigns, regardless of deistic philosophers, masonic statesmen, liberal parliaments and congresses, even if we do not comprehend the plans of His world government. But it is clear as crystal and all the optimists of the world cannot deny it: Today Christ the King does not rule in public life.

The church towers, signs of a believing past, marks of inde-structible, surviving belief under the surface of materialism, pro-phetic index fingers of a coming period of Christ the King, change nothing of the fact that the picture of the world in general, the po-litical, economic, cultural picture of the world is not Christian to-day, but rather materialistic and pagan. Deism has won. The cross on the orb has disappeared. Naturalism has triumphed. Politics ig-nores Jesus. Liberalism has won.

It looks as though the world in its centrifugal flight from Christ the King has reached its goal. But it is not yet at the end of the road. As the Holy Father pointed out, there is yet a fourth stage of god-lessness. It is the stage of violent atheism in both its forms: the god-lessness of tyranny and the godlessness of barbarity. Freedom emancipated from God, Christ and the Church will finally and nat-urally become a beast which mercilessly crushes everything that stands in its way. It will become the beast of hatred of God, because it recognizes God as the natural enemy of evil. It will become the beast of the Antichrist, because Christ came into the world in order to destroy the work of the devil. It will become the beast of perse-cution of the Church, because the Church is the guardian of mo-rality, conscience, authority, private property, the family, human dignity and the true rights of man.

Let us not deceive ourselves: We are on our way to Moscow! Moscow is the death of freedom, slavery under a handful of tyrants, the time when one is bound hand and foot and where weeping and gnashing of teeth in the utmost darkness become reality. Hell on earth! We're going to Moscow. That is not a prophecy. That is sim-ply the logic of world history, The connection is a matter of cause and effect. Christ is the Way. Whoever loses the Way falls into the abyss. Christ is the Truth. Whoever loses the Truth falls into dark-ness. Christ is the Life. Whoever runs away from Life finds death. That applies to the nations as well as to the individual. Moscow is the abyss, darkness, the death of the modern peoples who have be-come liberal.

However, I do not believe that Moscow will be the grave of mankind. I believe that mankind will be resurrected from the dead. After people have recognized that it is a matter of natural law that the flight from Christ the King leads to disaster, they will return to

Jesus. I believe, and I support my argument on the declarations of the popes, that before us lies a magnificent age of Christ the King. Christ triumphs! Christ rules! Christ reigns! It is the providential purpose of the Feast of Christ the King to prepare the minds and hearts of mankind for this wonderful future.

That is why we oppose the deist, naturalist, liberal slogan "Away with the King!" with another: "Back to Christ the King!" Back to Christ the King of souls! Back to Christ the King of the family! Back to Christ the King of the nations! Back to Christ the King of kings and Lord of lords! Long live Christ the King!

THE CRIME OF KEEPING SILENCE

It is wartime. World war. It is a world war of the spirit which followed the world wars of the bodies. Only blind, deaf and dumb souls do not yet know this. Two armies are fighting today for world domination, without making any bones about their wanting to conquer the whole world: Rome and Moscow. Both have published their slogans. The slogan of Rome is "The Kingdom of Christ!" The slogan of Moscow is "Away from God!" It is no longer a question of dogma or of individual articles of faith. It is no longer the battle between Church and heresy as in previous centuries. It is a battle for the whole, for everything: for Christ, for God, between heaven and hell.

It is impossible to find a motto that would say everything in a word about these two opponents. The kingdom of Christ is the radical and universal reign of God. Godlessness is the radical and universal reign of Satan. The one is the absolute opposite of the other. The godless movement, the social atheism of our days, was only possible because the understanding of the social kingship of Jesus had disappeared from public life. On the other hand, the movement of the godless, the great deluge, can only be overcome through a mighty, deep movement for the kingship of Christ among the people. Either social kingship of Christ or social atheism!

The reign of Christ over human society is endangered by two factors: the godlessness of Bethlehem's silence and the godlessness of Herod's hatred. In other words: the godlessness of laicism and the godlessness of Bolshevism; the godlessness of the Occident and the godlessness of Russian barbarism; the godlessness of man and the godlessness of the devil. On the Feast of Christ the King one must speak of both. The danger comes from the east, but the danger also comes from the west.

THE GODLESSNESS OF BETHLEHEM'S SILENCE, THE GREAT DANGER TO THE SOCIAL REIGN OF JESUS IN THE OCCIDENTAL WORLD

There is a silence about Christ the King as a matter of principle. Since 1789 this principle has formed the basis of the modern constitutions. The principle says: The state as such is non-denominational. It acts as though God would not exist, and as though the human being were God. Since religion is thus a private affair and only a private affair, the parliaments, governments and courts in their laws, decrees and decisions must be independent of conscience and the Gospel. Whether there is a God, whether Christ exists and whether He is King of society, whether the Church is a divine institution or not, all this is an exclusively religious matter and thus has nothing to do with politics. Therefore we shall not speak of it.

According to this theory, for the modern states consisting of believers and non-believers, Christians and Jews, Catholics and non-Catholics, there can be only one attitude toward religion: that of social atheism, of keeping silence as a matter of principle. Taken seriously, the social reign of Jesus is for the modern state specifically unconstitutional. There can be no doubt: such a principle is godless. It is not yet the godlessness of blasphemy and persecution, but it is godlessness in the fullest sense of the word. It is social deicide.

There is a silence about Christ the King as a matter of tactics. The modern non-denominational state has its eager students. Today they are organized preferably on the basis of religious neutrality. Whether in fact there can be such a thing as religious neutrality or not is another question. Here I am only stating the fact that the preferred organizational form is religiously neutral, non-denominational. What is neutrality, presupposing that it is not lack of character?

He who is neutral keeps his principles, provided that he has any, to himself. He also lets the others have theirs; to each his own. He is neither for nor against belief in God, in order not to hurt the feelings of the unbelievers. He is neither for nor against Christianity, in order not to insult the Jews. He is neither for nor against Catholicism, in order not to offend the heretics. The tactics of neutrality are the tactics of silence. They ignore the reign of Jesus over society. Nevertheless, as the Holy Father says, "the human beings united in the society stand no less under the power of Christ, than they do as individuals." Non-denominationlism is the opposite of the kingship of Christ.

There is silence about Christ the King out of cowardliness. There is no arguing against the fact that modern Catholicism is glad to proclaim its faith on official occasions and knows how to demonstrate it brilliantly. However, when it is a matter of representing the never outdated rights of Christ the King over public life as a minority against a majority, as subject against temporal rulers, as representative of so-called obsolete, unmodern views against the spirit of the times, then we lack what Bismarck once called civil courage.

Like Peter at the watchmen's fire, we have not the courage to stand up for an abandoned, betrayed, bound, mocked and crucified King. We are ashamed of the Lord of heaven and earth. If we do not directly deny Him, at least we are silent when His honor is called into question. We are cowards, despite Baptism and Confirmation.

The *Fides intrepida* (fearless faith) in Rome branded this "accursed silence" for what it is in the encyclical *Quas Primas*: "The more the most sweet Name of our Savior is passed over in silence at international conventions and in the parliaments, the more it is necessary to cry it out all the louder and proclaim everywhere the rights of His royal power and dignity."

The silence of laicism, which has grown to epidemic proportions, the non-denominalism and Catholic fearfulness have created a certain God-empty and Christ-empty atmosphere, which one can describe as social God-lessness. *Contraria contrariis curantur*—illnesses must be healed through their opposites. In order to cure the epidemic silence about the kingship of Christ, we must become loud, Catholic criers everywhere, heralds of the Great King.

A WORD ABOUT THE GODLESSNESS OF HEROD'S HATRED, THE GREAT DANGER TO THE SOCIAL KINGSHIP OF JESUS FROM THE NORTHEAST

Besides the cold godlessness of the Occident exists a flaming godlessness, the godlessness of hate. *Deus caritas est*—God is love. God is the One Who loves. Jesus is the One Who loves. The Catholic Church is one who loves. The devil is the one who hates, the ultimate God-hater and man-hater.

These two principles of love and of hate run through the entire history of the world, from the fall of man to the final judgment: the empire of love in battle against the empire of hate, and the empire of hate in battle against the empire of love.

However, there is development: love grows, and hatred grows. Love becomes ever more divine, while hatred becomes more and more devilish. If the Revolution of 1789, the mother of all modern revolutions, gave to error and to evil full civil rights guaranteed by the constitution, then we know where the logic of history must finally lead. The mother of the great revolution and of the modern rights of man is not love of freedom for all, but rather hatred of the exclusive rights of truth and virtue, hatred of the Great Monarch Who shares His throne with no other. From the very beginning, modern revolution is war against the social and universal world reign of Jesus. It is anti-Christian, godlessness not only in the negative, but in the positively hostile sense of the word.

The tree of social atheism, social Antichristianity, which was planted in that August night in Paris, 1789,[3] was raised to full maturity by Moscow. Moscow, that means hatred of Christ the King pure and undiluted, in its entirety: 100% hatred, which armed itself for a new slaughter of the innocents, a new Good Friday, in order to destroy Christianity with its last vestiges on the Golgotha of the west. It will not utter its *consummatum est*—it is finished, until the world has become God-less in the fullest sense of the word.

That is the question today, and that will be the question tomorrow: Who will be lord of the world? Christ the King? or the incarnation of the devil, the incarnate godlessness? We must arm for this mighty and decisive battle. It will be the time of the great apostasy, the time of the discernment of spirits. The halfhearted, the cowards and the cold will become betrayers. Only the wholehearted, those who possess the *fides intrepida*—the fiery soldiers, will endure.

---

[3]   Aug. 27, Declaration of the Rights of Man. [Translator's note.]

These are the people of Christ the King. And they will triumph over the blood-red dragon and his godless followers. They will then sing in all the alleyways and roads the song of Christ the King: "Christ Jesus, Victor! Christ Jesus, Ruler! Christ Jesus, Lord and Redeemer!"

NEUTRALITY OR THE KINGSHIP OF CHRIST?

Today nearly all states in Europe are constitutionally non-denominational. Once upon a time it was different. There was a time when the nations of the western world bore the sign of Christianity on their foreheads with pride and thankfulness. Then came the centuries of the decline of faith, the age of reason, Liberalism, Socialism. As Leo XIII remarked in his encyclical on Christian government, new rights began to gain in validity and dominance. Supposedly they were achievements of the maturity and progress of the peoples.

The modern states have declared themselves non-denominational. Religion is left to the individual as his private concern. However, the state as state proclaims official neutrality toward God, Christ and the Church. Non-denominationalism or religious neutrality of society has become the mark of the modern state, the actual social sin of the century and mother of all the other social sins of the century. We reject religious neutrality as a sin against common sense, character and religion.

Religious neutrality is a sin against common sense. Religious neutrality is renunciation of common sense. Religious neutrality is a declaration of the bankruptcy of the thinking brain. Whoever proclaims neutrality in the area of religion shows that he either understands nothing of the most important facts and truths of heaven and earth, or that he cannot distinguish between true and false, or that he considers yes and no, light and darkness, day and night, truth and error to be equals.

In the first case it is the neutrality of ignorance; the second is the neutrality of a mental handicap; the third is the neutrality of indifferentism. Regardless of to which type this intellectual neutrality on matters of religion belongs, it is the sign of a degenerate, senile time. Strong, healthy periods know nothing of neutrality. They have strong convictions, definite Yes and definite No, a clear For and an unambiguous Against. Intellectual neutrality, fundamental lack of conviction is a sin against common sense.

Religious neutrality is a sin against character! Character implies wholeness, a harmonious personality, agreement between belief and deed. Every person should form a complete unity, should speak and live as he thinks and think as he speaks and lives. That means unequivocal truthfulness! Inside and outside the same! And now, what does neutrality do? It divides the human being into two parts, an inner man and an outer man, a world of ideas and convictions on the one hand and a world of words and works on the other.

Then says neutrality: "At home in your inner world you can do as you like. You don't need to be neutral there. You can't be it, either. The heart is never neutral. The heart loves or hates, rejoices or mourns, hopes or fears, but it is not neutral. For the outside world, however, you have to hide your convictions or at least dilute them. You have to speak and behave as though you had either no conviction or another one than that which you have. You must respect every so-called honest opinion, no matter how nonsensical and dangerous it may appear to you. Let your own unalterable principle in public life be lack of principle. You must be neutral." We can see that neutrality is a school of lack of character.

Religious neutrality is a sin against religion! Neutrality appears in three forms: neutrality toward God, neutrality toward Christ, neutrality toward the Church. Neutrality toward God is practiced out of consideration for the atheists, the materialists and the pantheists; neutrality toward Christ out of consideration for the Jews; neutrality toward the Church out of consideration for the non-Catholics.

Neutrality toward God: God is the endlessly perfect Spirit, Lord of heaven and earth. Everything was made through Him. In Him all living things live and move and have their being. He is the All-Present, the Almighty, the All-Holy One. He is our Father. He is Love. Yet what does neutrality say about this God? "Let's not talk about Him in the legislative assemblies, in our negotiations, in our courts. We don't need Him. God must not interfere in the affairs of the nations. In any case, we cannot recognize His sovereignty over land and people. Sovereignty rests with the people." That is the language of thanklessness, of disrespect, of rebellion against the Most High. Neutrality against God is a crime against religion!

Neutrality toward Christ: Christ is the Lord, also Lord of the peoples. The nations are His inheritance. The ends of the earth are His property. On His belt is written: King of kings. Furthermore, He died out of love for us all and redeemed us through His precious Blood. What does neutrality toward Christ say about all that? "Officially we cannot recognize His spiritual sovereignty over our parliaments and governments. We leave Him the temples of our country as a free zone, but we cannot allow Him to reign over us." That's neutral language. Every atheist can have his fun with it. But it is not just neutral, it is nasty as well. Neutrality of baptized persons toward Christ is treason.

Neutrality toward the Church: The Church is not some private human association. She is the work of God, Christ living on, mediatrix of supernatural grace and truth, the mother and educator of the human race. What does neutrality toward the Church say in spite of this? It treats her like one or another religious sect, praises her perhaps now and then as servant of the state, protectress of the throne and the treasury, as a useful schoolteacher and charitable worker. But as far as the main issue is concerned, it denies or ignores the mother as queen. It denies her spiritual rights of sovereignty over state and society. To the queen and mother we owe respect, love and obedience, not neutrality. Neutrality toward a mother is disrespect, indifference, rebellion. Neutrality toward religion becomes sin against religion.

One final thought: Religious neutrality is an impossibility. No one can serve two masters. Either he will hate the one and love the other, or he will be subject to the one and despise the other. That is God's word and therefore an article of faith. One can love and honor all men regardless of differences. One should do it, also. One can and may and should do it, because that which all of us have in common must be loved and respected over and above all differences, namely our human dignity as creatures created in God's image, our common brotherhood and our common redemption. That is not serving two masters.

But what one can not, may not and should not do is to keep benevolent silence or to benevolently respect two inimical oppo-

sites: true and false, good and evil. Everyone, whether as statesman
or teacher or member of the board of directors or writer or father
of a family, will repeatedly fall out of the neutral role, whether he
or she wants to or not, and betray that which one really is: Catholic,
Protestant, liberal or socialist. There are no neutral governments,
no neutral schools, no neutral press, no neutral clubs, no neutral
families. The personality triumphs again and again over lack of
character, principle over diplomacy, the service of one master over
neutrality.

This applies to the life of nations! Periods of neutrality are periods of transition, of groping indecision. They are times of twilight
between day and night. After the time of neutrality comes the time
of service of one master, in which either Christ or Satan will be
king. After the liberal twilight comes either the Russian night of
persecution or the new Sun-Day of the Kingdom of Christ.

This is what we want to prepare. Therefore let us go and make
Christ King, first King of our minds and King of our hearts, then
King of our families and finally King of human society. The encyclical of Pius XI on the kingship of Christ must not have been written in vain. Christ must become King!

HOMESICKNESS FOR THE KINGDOM

The question of the century is whether Christ shall be King.
The kingship of Christ is the stone which the liberal builders have
rejected and which, according to the encyclical of Pius XI has become again the cornerstone of a new age. All architects of the future, whether they work in the areas of science or art, politics or
economics, morality or religion, will have to refer to the encyclical
Quas Primas.

Otherwise they will be "like a foolish man, that built his house
upon the sand. And the rain fell, and the floods came, and the
winds blew, and...that house...fell, and great was the fall thereof"
(Mt. 7:26-27). "For other foundation no man can lay, but that
which is laid; which is Christ Jesus" (I Cor. 3:11). "And whosoever
shall fall on this stone, shall be broken: but on whomsoever it shall
fall, it shall grind him to powder" (Mt. 21:44). Either there will be

the reconstruction of the kingdom of Christ, or there will be a general collapse! To be or not to be, that is the question today.

One senses now that it is a question of greatest, of utmost importance, of all or nothing. It lies like the atmosphere of Advent over mankind. There is great anxiety among the people because of the stormy thundering of the sea. Yet there is also longing and desire for the strong Redeemer, the coming King. We have had enough of the liberal era with its rights of man, its limitless arbitrariness and its God-empty laicism. We demand once again an Era of the Rights of God. We are sick of the wild anarchy in questions of truth and morals. We want law and order once again. We are tired of the harsh dictatorship of the spirit of the times, of the masses, of the wallet and the lodge. We demand a return of the mild reign of the Crucified! Christ must be King!

There must be homsickness for the kingdom of Christ in the intellectual realm! It has become dark and dreary and empty in the world of the thoughts, as after a hurricane, an earthquake, a flood. Everywhere there are ruins and rubble. There is nothing certain, nothing concluded, nothing recognized, except within the Church. There is no ground on which to stand, no rock on which to build, no way that one can follow, nowhere to stop along the way. There are only riddles, problems, hypotheses, questions, doubts, only dissolution, splintering, divisions, sects, confusion, anarchy. The Sun of Truth disappears more and more completely behind the sea of fog and clouds which is ignorance. Night is falling, disconsolate, eerie night, despite that great power, the press, despite the mountains of literature, despite the thousands of palatial schools.

It can't go on this way. Someone has to come and say: Let there be light! A King over the realm of thought! One Who proclaims the whole, infallible truth with divine authority! One Who cannot err and cannot be deceived! The King of the realm of intellect, Christ! Christ must again be recognized as King of Truth by all the scholars, professors, writers and editors; He must be honored, heard and called upon, as King, I say, as Sovereign of human intelligence.

Only when Christ is again acclaimed King over the realm of thought, will Truth no longer be a trembling beggar before the world, but rather a queen. No longer will it be merely tolerated and be granted the same constitutional rights as error, but will be a monarch, no longer a weak construction of one's own mind or feeling, but ruler over the person, setting the standards for all and obliging all to respect it. Christ must be King over the realm of thought, if truth should once again triumph over error and falsehood.

There must be a longing for Christ as King of the realm of the will!

There is only one centerpoint in a circle. There is only one center of the universe, from Which all things proceed and to Which all things return. The universe does not exist under the sign of democracy, but of monarchy, not oligarchy but of exclusive kingship! There is only one God. There is only one sovereign, almighty Will, Whom all others must serve, in this way or that, whether they want to or not. Contrary to this has arisen an erroneous teaching in the universe, the mother of all other errors: sin.

Sin says: "There is more than one middle in the circle, more than one center in the universe! There is more than one sovereign will! There is more than one God! Everything is God! Every person is God! I, too, am God! I, too, can do what I want to!" Sin denies the monarchy in the universe, the divine monarchy. Particularly modern times have set up, by means of Liberalism and laicism, the principle: "Not God alone is Center of public life, but the state, the people, the citizen! Man is ruler over himself!" The essence of the liberal sin is thus rebellion against the sovereign, universal Monarchy exercised by Christ, the reign of the Most High over heaven and earth, governments and people, Church and state.

Nothing is more necessary today than to oppose the liberal sin, the "pest of laicism," as Pius XI called it, with the Biblical and Catholic truth of the exclusive monarchy of one most high Sovereign, who rules over all and everything. This providential task fills out the idea of Christ the King. Like a new Moses from the Sinai of the Vatican Hill, Pius XI proclaimed that Christ rules in the entire kingdom of the will! Christ has power over all temporal things! Christ is Lord of civil society! Christ rules over the entire human race! Christ has received from the Father absolute rights over all creatures! Christ is King of kings and Lord of lords, therefore the Monarch of the universe, sole ruler of the universe and heir of all things (Heb. 1:1)! That is the great Catholic thesis, which the Feast of Christ the King opposes to the liberal thesis. That is the Catholic program for the century: restoration of the divine monarchy in creation through Christ the King in the entire realm of human will. There must be a longing for Christ the King in the realm of the heart! God can accelerate the restoration, extension and fortification of Christ's universal monarchy by extraordinary means. He can break with His iron scepter the liberal potters' vessels and the modern idols. But the positive building of Christ's kingdom of peace can only come about through the great power of love. The sun of truth shining from the face of Jesus is not sufficient. Not even the iron rod of awesome majesty will do it alone. The world will not convert after it is beaten and convinced. It may not even be converted after its arrogance has been smashed by the penalties imposed upon it. It will only convert after it has recognized that despite its sins it is loved by God with endless love. The heart of the King makes greater, more numerous and more lasting conquests than the King's head and arm.

Homesickness for Christ's kingdom of the heart—perhaps this homesickness is still too weak in many places. The great herd is still running after other gods. But none of these gods will satisfy its thirst for love, neither Bacchus, god of addiction to enjoyment and pleasure, nor Mercury, god of greed, nor Venus, goddess of sensual lust, nor any of the "idols of gold, and silver, and brass, and stone, and wood, which neither can see, nor hear, nor walk" (Apoc. 9:20). The heart remains cold and empty and unsatisfied, even if it were to drink up whole oceans of so-called joys.

And suddenly, out of the depths of the terrible need of the modern soul, rises up the longing for the Only One who can fill the heart completely, the longing for Jesus. Then they will go and make Him King. Then there will be peace on earth—only then. *Pax Christi in regno Christi*—the peace of Christ in the kingdom of Christ. On that day we shall not just be Catholic because it is sensible to be Catholic, not even because we are afraid of not dying Catholic; instead we will be Catholics because Catholicism is the kingdom of Love, and Christ is the Prince of the kingdom of Love. That will be the great discovery of the century, the King of the peoples Who was lost through the liberal sin, forgotten but now rediscovered, Jesus Who is Love!

The question of Christ the King is the great question of the century! Therefore do what you do on the Feast of Christ the King wholeheartedly. The idea of Christ the King is no solemn lie, no empty phrase, no theatrical production, but rather a holy and inviolable vow! Christ must be King! Christ must triumph! Christ must rule! Christ must reign! At first He must reign within, in the realm of thought, will and heart; then, however, He must reign outside in the family, the state and society. That October 31 more than four hundred years ago[4] was the signal for the social apostasy of western Christianity from the universal kingship of Christ. The last Sunday in October should be today the signal for the return of the peoples to their King. One God, one Christ, one King, one Realm!

BACK TO THE GREAT ONE

There are two mysterious forces in the world, in the material world as well as the spiritual world: the power of attraction and the power of flight, the attraction to the center and the flight from the center. The scholars call them centripetal and centrifugal forces. The centerpoint of all things is God, the King. The centripetal force of the spirit must strive toward Him through faith, hope and love. The centrifugal force away from the King acts through unbelief, erroneous belief, desperation, hatred of God, in general through every sin.

Thanks to October 31, 1517, the religious centrifugal force in the European peoples found its theological system. It is Protestantism. Protestantism is the flight from the divine center in the field of religion. Then came Liberalism. Liberalism is the flight from the divine center in the political field. Capitalism is the flight from the divine center in the area of economics. The end of the untrammeled religious, political and social flight of Protestantism, Liberalism and Capitalism is the freezing, dissolution and death of society.

And now we observe how modern mankind in its race toward death by petrification and asphyxiation, demonstrates a remarkable reaction. The natural fear of death, the drive for self-preservation

---

[4] On Oct. 31, 1517, Luther published his theses in Wittenberg.
[Translator's note.]

has unleashed the centripetal force once again. Protestantism, Liberalism and Capitalism, the three outward forms of human individualism with its aversion to a midpoint, no longer satisfy wide parts of society. They are again in search of the lost center. They once more look for the unified center of their thinking, their will, their lives. They want to get away from the variety and miscellany of individualism.

It would seem that the divine attraction of grace is working toward the world kingdom of the great King, the one Shepherd and the one flock.

The future should be under the sign of the great One: one Lord, one faith, one Baptism, one God and Father of all, one body and one Spirit (*Cf.* Eph. 4:4-6). Catholic centripetal force replaces Protestant-liberal-capitalist centrifugal force!

There is only one God and Father of all! Immeasurably rich is the world of the air, the water and the earth, populated by numberless living things, by over 200,000 types of plants and 500,000 species of animals. Beyond this is the universe of stars with its millions and billions of heavenly bodies. Yet in this entire, immeasurable universe science finds the same materials and the same laws. There is only one mathematics, one mechanical science, one physics and one chemistry in the universe. Creation is a unified whole, the work of One. There is only one God and Father of all, "who is above all, and through all, and in us all" (Eph. 4:6).

Monotheism, the belief in one God above all gods, the idea of a single Cause of all other causes, is the foundation and cornerstone of religion. Though it be overgrown and buried under idol worship and superstition, there is still deep in the soul of man, even in the pagan peoples, this notion of the One and Only, the God and Father of all. Livingstone, the explorer of Africa, wrote: "One must not preach the existence of God even to the most degenerate Negro tribe. This truth is generally recognized in Africa." Max Muller, a historian of religion, said: "The more deeply we penetrate the past, the purer do we find the idea of the Deity." Polytheism is a product of later decadence.

Even for pagan peoples, before all and above all stands the great One. The catechism teaches us the highest wisdom when it places this great One vividly in the middle of the soul. There is only one

God! One Father of all! One highest Lawgiver! One center of all things! One final goal! The life of man, his thinking, willing and action, must be centripetal, in the direction of the great One. We are on earth in order to recognize God, to love God, to serve God. Therefore back to the great One according to the sense of the greatest commandment! Back to the Father.

There is only one Lord and King! God the One and Only, the Eternal and Omnipresent, can not be seen with the earthly eye. He "inhabiteth light inaccessible" (I Tim. 6:16). He is the Invisible. But the Invisible has become visible in Jesus Christ through His assumption of human nature. Jesus Christ is the midpoint of the universe and of world history. He is Alpha and Omega, A and Z, Beginning and End, the First and the Last (*Cf.* Apoc. 1:8). He is the Head and the Heart and the Soul of creation. As St. Paul, teacher of the peoples, says, He is "above all principality, and power, and virtue, and dominion, and every name that is named, not only in this world, but also in that which is to come" (Eph. 1:21). All visible and invisible beings, the angels and the human persons and the lower creatures, stand in absolute dependence upon the holy Humanity of the Lord, through Him, in Him, for Him. Christ is the great One in All! *Kyrios, Dominus*—the Lord! Creation is a monarchy ruled by Christ, the Great Monarch! One Realm, one King.

This monarchy, which is preached so emphatically in the letters of St. Paul, and which formed the basis of the early Christian and medieval world view, is denied, fought and forgotten, thanks to modern Liberalism. It is to Pius XI's eternal credit that through his encyclical on the kingship of Christ he hammered into the liberal world, especially the mighty of this earth, the fact of the monarchy of Christ over all things, including politics, economy, the arts and sciences. *Tu solus Dominus, tu solus Altissimus, Jesu Christe!* Thou alone art the Lord, Thou alone the Most High, Jesus Christ! Back to the great One in the world outlook!

There is only one Body! Through the Eastern Schism and the western fall from faith, Christianity has become divided. Today one speaks of Catholics, Orthodox and Protestants. One speaks of Christian confessions and even of "sister churches." This has become quite matter-of-fact, as though it had always been so. Yet nothing contradicts so much healthy common sense and the Gospels than to speak of "churches." Common sense says that there can be only one truth. The Gospel contradicts the plurality of churches, because Christ only founded one Church.

The Church founded by Christ is, however, more than a religious system and more than an organization. She is a living organism. She is the Mystical Body of Christ (*Cf.* Eph. 1:22-23). And Christ can only have one mystical Body, just as He has only one physical body. A head with more than one mystical body would be a monster, a congenital deformity. There may be many sects, but there can be only one Church of Christ. This one Church of Christ is the Catholic Church. She alone has the marks of truth: unity of faith, of liturgy and of government, holiness of moral doctrine and of the means of grace, universal extension and her age dating all the way back to the Apostles. The basic number of the Church is one! One head, one body, one Christ, one Church! One door, one Baptism, one truth, one faith! One creed, one confession!

Let us pray! The restoration of the general kingship of Christ is the work of God and not the work of men. For that reason it must be prepared more through prayer than through books and lectures. *Flectamus genua*—let us bend the knee! Let us wring out hands, let us raise eyes and hearts to the Holy Spirit, that like Pentecost the Reign of Christ come over us. Through Mary to the one God, to the one Lord and King and the one body which is the Church: Back to the great threefold One in the Kingdom of Christ!

MONARCHY

The kingdom of heaven is like a king....That means monarchy, even today. Modern humanity is antimonarchistic. First came the so-called Reformation and shook the throne of the spiritual king, the pope. Then came the revolution and shook the thrones of the political kings. Lastly came Liberalism and shook, together with its two sons, Socialism and Communism, the throne of God. Godless Russian Bolshevism was only the final phase of the antimonarchism that began with Luther. In the first place, it is not a matter of governmental reform. Governmental reform is another question entirely. It is in its deepest depths a revolutionary spiritual movement, a matter of the enthronement of the individual, the monarchy of the ego.

The slogan of Lutheranism is: Every man a pope! The slogan of modern revolution is: Every man a king! The slogan of radical Liberalism is, as a logical consequence: Every man a god! It was therefore really an epochal statement, embodiment of all pastoral work and of Catholic action, when the Holy Father Pius XI called out to the world: Long live Jesus the King! The universal kingship of Christ is the great Catholic thesis which we, whether we are monarchists or republicans, must oppose to the spirit of the times which is the enemy of authority. The kingdom of heaven is like a king.

Christ the King is the highest Lawgiver of the world! It was an extremely solemn moment, when the Resurrected Christ stood upon the mountain in Galilee. Before Him were the Apostles, the representatives of the young Church. Jesus came to them and said, "All power is given to me in heaven and in earth. Going therefore, teach ye all nations; baptizing them in the name of the Father, and of the Son, and of the Holy Ghost. Teaching them to observe all things whatsoever I have commanded you: and behold I am with you all days, even to the consummation of the world" (Mt. 28:18-20). That is the proclamation of the general, unlimited, eternal monarchy of Christ. Only One can be Possessor of all power, king in the fullest sense of the word: only He, only Jesus! Whoever has all power in heaven and in earth possesses the highest legislative power.

Modern mankind views every law as chains and bars for the free personality. In everyone who says to him, "Thou shalt," he sees an enemy. He has a morbid sympathy with all who mutiny and rebel, who criticize and deny, who revolt and foment uprisings, in short, with everything that carries the sign and seal of Lucifer in its heart and on its hand. He hates the law with its pure, inviolable majesty, wherever he meets it, whether in the universe or in his own breast, in the state and in the Church, in nature and in art. Yet without laws of chemistry and physics, nature becomes chaos; without the moral laws mankind becomes wild, uncontrollable confusion. Lawlessness would be the material, spiritual and moral downfall of the world. The law is that which must be, that which is sensible, useful, noble, beautiful, righteous, holy.

We speak of laws and lawgivers in the plural. Basically, however, there can be only one Lawgiver and only one law. We do not come from ourselves; we are made and created, all and everything. We exist because a Higher One wanted us to be. There is nothing made that was not made through Him, nothing that could even exist for one moment, if He had not brought it into existence. There is nothing that would take His place or could fulfill His commands without disturbing everything else, if He had not given it His laws and held them unfailingly valid. It follows from the nature of God as well as from the nature of all created things that God is the highest and only Lawgiver and the highest and only Law of all things.

If the world is to be and remain that which the Greek word *kosmos* and the Latin word *mundus* so beautifully express, namely a kingdom of harmony and order, and if the whole universe is not to collapse, then all must be under the rule of a single, absolute Lord. In the world of laws applies the principle: either monarchy or anarchy! Either there is one King, or there is dissolution and world conflagration!

The highest Lawgiver became Man. All legislative power of the Divinity was concentrated in Christ. To Him "all power is given" (Mt. 28:18), everything is through Him. "He is before all" (Col. 1:17). All peoples must observe all things whatsoever He has commanded (Mt. 28:20). Christ the highest Legislator of the nations! Christ the Law of the legislators! Christ the Norm of the parliaments! No law is law against His law. Every law that men pass is either through Him and in Him and for Him, or it is nothing. Christ the King must be highest Lawgiver of the World!

Christ the King is the highest government in the world! *Data mihi omnis potestas!* To me all power is given. That means the power of government as well! Donoso Cortés once said, "Today the governors of the nations can call themselves kings or presidents, but they do not reign. The governments cannot reign anymore, because the peoples have become ungovernable." In any case there are no more kings who truly reign today. The kings who have survived the storms of revolution are nothing but decoration and representation anymore. That is why it is comprehensible that modern liberal mankind has no more understanding for a God Who reigns. So-called deism may yet believe in the existence of a Supreme Being, but this highest Being is tied hand and foot when it comes to the laws and the affairs of the world. His name is Impotence.

Christ is also impotent in the eyes of the modern liberal world. He is no longer the Grand Monarch of the early Church, *Kyrios, Dominus, Imperator,* the King of kings, the Lord. The orb in His hand no longer symbolizes the great religious and political fact that Christ not only has the right of possession over the universe, but actually exercises the governing power over the world. By contrast, Pope Pius XI did not conjure up a medieval legend or a fantastic, futuristic dream with his encyclical on Christ the King, but rather confirmed a fact: I, the possessor of all power, am with you all days, even unto the consummation of the world.

Christ reigns! Not the prime ministers and not the parliaments, not big capital and not the press, not democracy and not the powers of hell! To rule means to bring to reality the goal of a realm. The goal of the divine world government is the kingdom of heaven. Through Christ the King, God wills to make of all who are of good will a realm of children of God, a kingdom of eternal glory and blessedness. To this supernatural end of the world all creatures must co-operate. All events are instruments of Providence! "For all things are yours," says St. Paul, "and you are Christ's" (I Cor. 3:22-23). In the hands of the Almighty, everything becomes a means of educating, purifying and sanctifying the children of God.

World history has the single purpose of populating the kingdom of heaven with saints, with martyrs and confessors, with virgins and penitents. And Christ will achieve this goal. Christ reigns! All heresies, all periods of decadence, all persecutions of Christians, all wars and revolutions will not prevent Him from it. Christ reigns. Not according to political principles, not from the standpoint of economic and business calculations, but according to pastoral principles as Priest does He rule. Yet there is no government that leads to its goal with so much wisdom and power, so much infallible certainty despite apparent mishaps, as the government of Christ the King. The obelisk on St. Peter's Square is right. "Christ triumphs, Christ reigns!" He is the King for Whom everything lives.

Christ the King, Judge of the world! Just as it is not enough to make laws, for they must also be enforced, so also it is not enough to reign and enforce them without also understanding how to judge. A government without a court would be just as useless as legislation without government. Now, the Gospel says, "For neither doth the Father judge any man, but hath given all judgment to the Son, that all men may honor the Son, as they honor the Father" (Jn. 5:22-23). You have to take Christ as He is. A sentimental, softly sweet Christ is no genuine Christ. The Gospel draws a picture of Christ with the features of manliness, strength and justice.

The Good Samaritan is also the severe Reprover. The Lamb led to the slaughter is also the Lion of the Tribe of Judah. The Proclaimer of the law of love for one's enemies is also the Prophet of the destruction of Jerusalem. Furthermore, if one wants to know the whole Christ, one must not only read the Gospel, but also the Apocalypse: Christ is the Judge! "And his eyes were as a flame of fire,...and his voice as the sound of many waters....And from his mouth came out a sharp two-edged sword..." (Apoc. 1:14-18). He has in His hand "the keys of death and of hell" (*ibid*) and thunder and lightning are the messengers of His throne.

Christ judges! There is a court that follows upon the heels of sin with a certain natural inevitability. It belongs to the wonderful institutions of divine justice that the violation of the law carries to a certain degree the punishment in itself. Everything evil is against common sense, ridiculous, unhealthy, damaging, suicidal, even when it does not take such obvious forms as gluttony, alcoholism or sexual immorality. As far as world history is concerned, one calls it world judgment. The mist arising from the sins of the peoples always comes back down on them in the form of catastrophes. Yet all this pales before the terrors of which the final Gospel of the Church year tells. And then, when we speak of Christ the King, we must call to mind the central prison of creation: There is a hell! A fire that is never extinguished! Christ, King of the world, is also Judge of the world!

Why doesn't Christianity today have any energy? Why is there no drive for greatness in us? Why are we almost always nothing but passengers and so seldom engineers or firemen on the locomotive? Why was Liberalism in the past, why is Socialism today called the locomotive of history Why shouldn't it be Catholicism again? Because we lack the great ideas that conquer the world. Or, better said, they lack us. The idea of Christ the King would be such a world-conquering and world-renewing slogan. That is what we must bring to the masses. That is what we have to give to the youth as its banner. In this way we could move mountains. Mexico showed us how an entire people marching under this banner[5] could become heroes, confessors and martyrs. Under this flag we shall also march into the coming decisive battle: Long live Christ the King!

QUEEN AND MOTHER

Since June 7, 1929, the Holy Father is the recognized sovereign of Vatican City, pope and king. The *Citta del Vaticano* may be the smallest kingdom in the world, but it is a kingdom, more so than all other monarchies on earth. Yet important as that day may be for the present and the future, its significance is far less than that of the day in Cesarea Philippi, which St. Matthew reports in his Gospel (Mt. 16:18-19), records the divine institution of the spiritual kingdom of St. Peter.

The pope is not just king because he is a worldly prince over so and so many square miles of territory, but above all because he is Peter and Christ built His Church upon this rock; because He gave him the keys to the kingdom of heaven; and because everything he binds on earth is bound in heaven and everything he looses on earth is loosed in heaven. Therefore he is a king, because he is established by God as head of the kingdom established by God! He is king because he is pope.

Three problems of kingship hang, stand and fall together: The problem of Christ's kingdom, the problem of the pope's kingdom and the problem of the Church's kingdom. The three are one, they

---

[5] Fr. Mäder refers here to the tragic Mexican revolution of 1911-1917, the aftermath of which brought bloody civil wars when the people rebelled against the suppression of the Church by the victorious masonic Party of Revolutionary Institutions (PRI). The battles still raged while Fr. Mäder was writing, and ended with the confiscation of Church property and severe repression of the Church since 1927. [Translator's note.]

are various aspects of one and the same thing. With his encyclical *Quas Primas*, Pius XI proclaimed not only the world reign of Jesus, but also the world-wide reign of the Church and of her head. As necessary as was the first thing, so timely was the other.

The plague of laicism condemned by the encyclical consisted exactly in the fact that for a hundred years the spiritual reign of the Church over public life of the states and peoples had been denied and contested under the domination of Liberalism. It was undesirable that the Church reign over us because it was undesirable that Christ reign over us.

Hostility towards the Church was, is and ever shall be Antichristianity.

That is why practical work for the kingship of Christ always consists precisely in the deepening and extension of the world-wide reign of the Church. Whoever is for the Queen is also for the King. And vice versa: Whoever is for the King, must also be for the Queen.

So the Church is a Queen! What a wonderful drama: The Holy Father had just given up his rights to the Papal States which were hallowed by a thousand years. He did not want any more worldly domination than his spiritual independence as head of Christendom demands. And then there came the Italian parliament and tried to grab away the sovereignty of the Church over the souls of her children. And the *Fides intrepida* suddenly leapt up like an angry lion! He who sacrificed a whole earthly kingdom became implacable, when the spiritual sovereignty of the Church was called into question. Thus the realm of the spirit, the sovereignty of the Church extends over and beyond the *Citta del Vaticano*, even unto the ends of the earth, over peoples and empires and souls.

That does not sound liberal, but it does sound like the Gospel. As Holy Scripture shows, Christ founded his Church as a kingdom, as a sovereign, universal monarchy with independent, lawgiving, reigning and judging power. The Monarch is and remains Jesus. The Church is Jesus living on. "Behold, I am with you all days, even to the consummation of the world" (Mt. 28:20). "Of his kingdom there shall be no end" (Lk. 1: 33). "Jesus Christ, yesterday, and to-day, and the same for ever" (Heb. 13:8).

However, there are two sides to this kingship. The kingdom is invisible and visible, divine and human, immortal and temporal at the same time. In accordance with the invisible aspect it is the kingdom of Christ; on the visible side it is the papacy and the ecclesiastical hierarchy. Yet however one may regard it, it is one and the same indivisible kingdom. "As the Father hath sent me, I also send you" (Jn. 20:21). "The Church has no less and no other kind of power than her King Jesus Christ," says Fr. A. M. Weiss. Between king and queen there is a spiritual community of property. Whatever the king owns and can do, the queen also owns and can do. "Always and everywhere, Christ and his Church are one and the same power, one and the same authority." (Fr. Weiss) The Church is Queen, because Christ is King!

The Church is Queen in the realm of truth, the teacher of the peoples! (*Cf.* Mt. 28:19). That is why she is also teacher of the teachers and shepherds of the peoples, of the princes and the governments. The modern state, the modern school and the modern media have contested the supreme right to educate the nations which Christ has conferred upon the Church. The Church can and perhaps may still exercise her teaching office, but only beside and perhaps below them, in any case not as sovereign, not as Queen. In place of the sovereignty of the teaching Church have arisen the sovereignty of government as teacher, science as teacher, journalism as teacher.

To everything its proper place! We are not so unmodern and intolerant as to want to shut the mouth of the state, the school and the press. They may well talk. But we are, as Pope Pius XI wrote, "not in accord with all that seeks to suppress, limit and contest that which nature and God have given the family and the Church in the area of education. In this respect we are intransigent." The Church is Queen in the realm of thought, pillar and bastion of truth and therefore teacher of all teachers including the state, the school and the media. "The nations die of hunger if the Church does not give them their daily bread," said Donoso Cortés. The Church is Queen of the realm of the will! It would be superstitious to regard law and commandment as an attack on human freedom. The reason for the commandment is not to be a chain and prison bars, but to be a road sign showing the way. Divine law is liberating and redemptive. It is the light, expression of that which is common sense, good, noble, just and useful, or else a warning sign against that which is offensive to God, senseless, bad, nasty, low, unjust and disastrous. Every God-given commandment or prohibition is a grace for which one ought to be thankful. That is why the sovereign lawgiving right of the Church is one of the greatest benefits for the human race. Only with it can one see where the path and where the chasm are. Only then does one know what one should do or should not do. The Spirit of God moved over the void and there was light.

The Church, Queen of the realm of the will! The Church is lawgiver of all laws, just as she is teacher of all teachers. That hurts modern pride, but it is so. He, to Whom all power is given in heaven and on earth, said in the most solemn moment before His Ascension into heaven: Teach them "to observe all things whatsoever I have commanded you" (Mt. 28:20). All things, everything! "All actions, insofar as they are good or bad from the standpoint of morals, *i.e.,* insofar as they are in accord with the natural and divine law or deviate from it, are subject to the judgment and the judicial office of the Church" (Pope St. Pius X, Encyclical *Singulari Quadam*).

That applies to everybody, without exception. That means the politicians as well! That means the academics! The artists! Even the businessman! Even the worker, female as well as male! Every action has a moral aspect, a side turned toward God or turned away from him, and accords or conflicts with the divine world order. Under this aspect (at least indirectly) it is subject to the sovereignty of the Church, the universal Queen in the realm of the will!

Now, if we only proclaim to the modern liberal world the queenship of the Church, it will not understand us. The modern world does not like thrones and crowns, least of all those of the only absolute monarchy, such as the Church is. So that one will understand us, we must also add the other attribute: Queen Church is also a mother. It is so easily forgotten that the state is the extended family, just as the family is the embryo of the state. The king is the father of the family which is his country, just as the father is king of the individual family. The deepest essence of kingship is fatherliness and motherliness! Devotion, sacrifice, service to all!

One of the most inspired statements of Donoso Cortés is: "Today more than ever, reigning is an act of self-denial, a noble sacrifice. In order to govern, it is not enough to be strong and just. In order to be truly strong and just, one must also be kind and lovable. Love is the virtue of the saints. Only saints can save the governments today." What Donoso Cortés demands of monarchs applies to every government: either one takes up one's office in order to be a father to the people, or one will be a tyrant. Either one governs, like St. Peter, in order to love more, serve more and sacrifice more than the others, or one becomes a betrayer of the highest office in the country.

Queen Church is mother as no other queen has ever been. She lives only in order to love. Whether she sacrifices, dispenses sacraments, preaches, commands, feeds the hungry or cares for the suffering, she always does the same thing: She loves! The best proof that motherliness is her most essential character trait is that her three favorites are the child, the poor and the sick. And whoever has these three witnesses on his side is irrefutable. Whoever has these three as his lawyers is unbeatable. Catholicism is love.

As opposing evidence one may point to the black pages in the Church's history, pages that tell of arrogance, imperiousness, greed or even brutality. The black pages speak against individual persons who were in the sanctuary but who dishonored it. But they do not speak against the Church. If you want to throw stones, then throw them at the guilty, at the sons who went wrong, but not at the mother. I repeat: Catholicism is love. It wants to reign, not in order to tyrannize, but in order to serve the peoples. The Church is Queen of the nations, but only in order to be their mother.

Queen Church is a mother! And in this mother's house is freedom and peace. The house of the mother is no prison, in which the children wear handcuffs and fetters. Catholics are neither slaves nor prisoners. On the contrary, no one is freer than they. Of course the Church is the sovereign, absolute, unlimited, divine authority. We live in God's will. But we live in God's will like the birds of the air and the fish in the water. If Catholicism were a prison, then one could also say that the bird and the fish are in prison, because the realm of air as well as that of water have their limits, at which they can go "thus far and no further." And yet it would occur to no sensible person to say such a thing.

Every being has its limits and laws, its "thus far and no further," that which it can do and that which it cannot. But no realm is less limiting for the exercise of our wills than Catholic air. Nowhere does one breathe more freely than in the realm of Catholic justice and love, because nowhere else does one leave to each his own and respect the rights of the stranger. In the realm of a Queen who is Mother, there is freedom and there is peace.

The Church must be Queen and Mother! The more she is both, the more certain is the welfare of the nations. For two centuries uninterrupted wars and revolutions have followed one another in order to usher in the era of general liberty, equality and brotherhood. All in vain! There is only one way to bring about a truly golden age of the nations, only one freedom which gives and secures for them all others, and without which all the others are nothing. The mother of all genuine freedom is the freedom of the Church!

Let the Church be that which she is, free Queen and Mother, and the face of the earth will be renewed. Proclaim in all lands the unlimited sovereignty of the Church, and all political and social problems will be solved. "God loves nothing more on this earth than the freedom of His Church."